THE "KAMIKAZE" EXPERIENCE
OF MIDLIFE CRISIS

THE "KAMIKAZE" EXPERIENCE OF MIDLIFE CRISIS

Ways To Deal With The Exceedingly Difficult World Of MLC

A Self-Help Guide For The Suffering Partner

Flash!

iUniverse, Inc.

New York Lincoln Shanghai

THE "KAMIKAZE" EXPERIENCE OF MIDLIFE CRISIS

Ways To Deal With The Exceedingly Difficult World Of MLC

iUniverse books may be ordered through booksellers or by contacting:

iUniverse
2021 Pine Lake Road, Suite 100
Lincoln, NE 68512
www.iuniverse.com
1-800-Authors (1-800-288-4677)

Because of the dynamic nature of the Internet, any Web addresses or links contained in this book may have changed since publication and may no longer be valid.

The views expressed in this work are solely those of the author and do not necessarily reflect the views of the publisher, and the publisher hereby disclaims any responsibility for them.

ISBN: 978-0-595-44087-0 (pbk)
ISBN: 978-0-595-88410-0 (ebk)

Printed in the United States of America

Dedication

To my wife, my darling, my (ex) partner. Know that I have always loved you. I know that I will love you forever. However, I am no longer in love with you. I cannot let myself be. That was your choice. You asked (rather told) me not to be. Your actions force me not to be. I bear you no malice. I acknowledge and accept my faults freely. I ask for your forgiveness and acceptance. I forgive you, and more than that I forgive myself too. You have helped me learn a great deal about us.

I have learned that life is a "roller coaster" with its ups, downs and dark tunnels. Some rides and thrills we shared together, others we may take on our own or with different partners. We are on separate paths and in different countries now. I do not know whether they will cross or join up again.

I do not regret one moment of the time we spent together. Of course there were times when we frustrated each other, but this went with the territory. We were meant to share at least part of this life side by side. Whether we join up again in this life or the next, I will always treasure the time we spent as a unit. Go now and be free, in peace!

And to my children, if you find this book on the back of a shelf or lying on a coffee table, know this, I still love you more than anything in this world. None of this is or ever was your fault. I so want you not to be affected by the break-up of our family and we are losing our frequent precious contact. I know that what has happened is affecting you now and will affect your attitude towards relationships in the future. I promise that as your father I will always be there for you as your best friend and that everything will be all right in the end.

To those who ask "Would I take my partner **back**?" I answer, "No, not now. It takes two willing partners to make a relationship work. If she ever chooses to discuss the possibility of reconciliation, I don't know whether I will be in a position or want to share the rest of my life with this new person." Rather I will say, "**I** might choose to go **forward** with her if and when the time is right."

This might be the same for you. Read on, and all will become clear!

This book is not intended to bore you with my personal story, although I too have been greatly affected by the effects of Midlife on both me and my spouse. It has obviously changed my thinking and educated me in many ways. This is more of a general guide so that others may benefit from techniques and strategies that are discussed.

I would also to like to thank my great friends Tower (for editing), Pippy and Sparkles, who have given greatly of their time and effort to help me get over my loss and encouraged me to complete this labour of love.

CONTENTS

Chapter 1:   Introduction 1

Chapter 2:   Before (The Happy Years?) 30

Chapter 3:   The Beginning (Is There A Storm On The
Horizon?) 33

Chapter 4:   Middle (The Crisis) 38

Chapter 5:   Detaching with Love (Probably The Jointly Most
Important Step!) 73

Chapter 6:   Other Strategies (Ways To Cope) 84

Chapter 7:   The End (Is The Sun Coming Out Again?) 104

Chapter 8:   After The End (Is There Life After The "Death?").. 109

Chapter 9:   Abbreviations, Quotes And Jokes........................... 111

Chapter 10: Finale 140

A Final Laugh 143

Update (June 2007) 145

About the Author.. 147

Index Of Selected Questions 149

A Note About Style

I have written this book as if I was actually with you, sitting on your couch or across the table with a cup of tea or coffee. That is why the punctuation is as it is, with comma breaks for breath! You will note I have used a lot of s/he and her/him references in the book. This has been in an attempt to personalise your situation, to make it easy to apply to **you**. It might seem confusing at first, but I promise you will get used to it! I will also attempt to give both views in answer to some questions, firstly from the LBS'er (Left Behind Spouse) point of view, and then from the MLC'er (Midlife Crisis'er).

MLC—"Midlife Crisis" or "My Life's Crap"

Whatever you think about it, wherever you live, however you have been brought up or educated, whether you believe in the theory or practice of a Midlife Crisis or not, there is undoubtedly something big happening to you now that has to be dealt with. Whether you want to or not, in this instance you do not have a choice. You may not have heard of or believe in the theory of Midlife Crisis, nor be able or willing to accept that there may be a rational explanation for what is happening between you and your loved one.

If you are going through this life changing experience yourself, you might not believe that you are having a crisis at all, just think that your whole attitude is changing (maybe going through "Transition"), that your life could be better in some way or other and now be determined to make it so, regardless of the consequences. So, to the recently deserted or abandoned spouse, we may choose to term what is happening a "Midlife Crisis." The MLT'er or MLC'er might just see it another way and think or have thought "My Life is Crap."

Whatever the case, I will try to give you some background and ways of understanding and coping with what may now seem like the most drastic of changes that are occurring in this period of your life.

A Note For "Newbie" LBS'ers

If you are in your thirties or older and have just found your relationship to be in transition or crisis, like most of us at the start you probably don't know where or who to turn to for help. You might, if you are lucky, have started marriage counselling, either jointly or on your own. You might not have a partner willing to participate, but you want to know what is happening, what to do, and may have decided to save your relationship if at all possible.

If you are new to the concept of Midlife Transition or Crisis and are just starting to experience its effects, your head may be spinning around so much at the moment that it is difficult to focus on anything, let alone read a lengthy book. You may have so many thoughts rushing round your head that you feel in a total muddle or mess. Take your time, breathe deeply, relax as much as you can and just read as much as you are willing to. Don't try to take it all in at once. Come back whenever you are ready. This book is here to help you, not make your problems seem even worse than they are. If you can't wait and want a specific question answered right now, turn to the back of the book and look at the index of selected questions to try and see if it is included and where to find an answer.

A Note For "Advanced"LBS'ers

You might be aware of a lot of what is in this book. However, during my journey I have discovered a great deal more than was available to me at first. I believe that what I discovered initially may have been restrictive, leaving out a lot about relationships that could or should have been considered and brought into the mix. For this reason I have included information that you may wish to give thought to, perhaps at a later stage or in retrospect.

Many "mid-range" MLCer's will actually believe that nothing is fundamentally "wrong." Of course s/he might have experienced radical thought changes and is fully conscious of them, even having some depression, but at some stage everything seems to come right. The decisions made or actions taken make sense. In fact, s/he may only be partway through the "Transition" process, although s/he might think it is over. It is only later as further progression through the stages is made that proper understanding and realisation of what has happened and is taking place seems to shock her/him back into another forced temporary or permanent reality.

A Note For MLC'ers

What are you doing and how did you get here? I do hope you have found this book as a result of your own questions and search, because **you** want to find possible reasons for your actions for yourself. Be assured that what you are going through is a "natural" aging process. Whatever state you are in, please bear in mind that your partner is probably going through "hell" right now and only trying to do the right thing in "awful" circumstances. Whatever you choose to read, please note that this has been written for your partner to try and cope with whatever you may be doing that affects her/him and others. Nothing that you may read justifies bad, cruel or insulting behaviour under any circumstances.

On the other hand, you may not be fully aware of the effect you are having at the moment. Perhaps you will find out a lot about how your actions are affecting others, and this may make you more sympathetic to their plight. Do not just dismiss the best-attempted actions of others that still care for **you**!

The Intention Of This Book

The intention of this book is to provide you (the LBS'er) with information that will allow **you** to regain control of **your** life. You may wish to save your relationship. You may not. It may not be possible. There are no guarantees of success. That does not mean you shouldn't try and give it your best shot if **you** want to. Just know and learn when to stop hurting yourself anymore. However, saying all that, there are time-tested strategies that work a lot better than others. Just remember that you have to put **yourself** first now. Do not think for a moment that you can or should control the actions of another. It may have gone so far that you could already be sleeping apart or living separately.

My best advice is to prepare for the worst possible outcome and expect nothing more. Then, whatever the eventual result, it can only be the same or better! That is not to say you must think negatively. Always maintain a positive attitude if and when you can. Be realistic and don't fall into the trap of creating or having false hopes. Easy to say, I know, but this will come with time.

This book is not intended to be a "one-time" read. I hope that you will come back to it time and time again, that it will become your "repeat prescription!"

A Word Of Advice

Take whatever you want from this book, and ignore what you don't like, is not appropriate or can't use! That's my guide for what you are about to read. Even though a lot of what is written here may seem to make a lot of sense straight away, it might not all apply to your particular circumstances, or at least you might think it doesn't at the moment. MLC is a very personal experience. That is why everything that is written here is from a singular perspective. However, individual situations may or may not apply to you. As you develop power and become in control of yourself from now on, **you** decide!

Disclaimer

There is an important disclaimer and proviso to everything you will read. I am neither a professional lawyer nor a doctor. I am a fellow "sufferer" or "victim." The information provided is just that, it is not a set of instructions that you have to follow. They cannot be guaranteed to work for you. For medicinal, legal or counselling issues, please contact professionals for their advice and guidance before proceeding with any course of action, and do not be tempted to do anything illegal!

MLT v MLC or MLW!

I believe it is very important to note, right here and now, that there is a difference between MLT (Midlife Transition) and MLC (Midlife Crisis.) All of us go through transition at various stages of our lives. This is totally natural. We question who and where we are, what we are doing and what we might like to do in the future. Many cope with this question and answer period in the most mature way and accept their fate with open arms. Some choose to change just one aspect of their lives. Others want to alter everything, creating chaos for everyone else along the way. These are "Crisis candidates". Be very careful before slotting your partner straight away into the "Crisis" category! But, more of this later.

On the other hand, and I have to thank "Tower" for this, your partner might be going through MLW. This stands for "Midlife Woteva!" Bearing in mind the "Teenage" mind influence and whether s/he is going through Transition or causing mayhem or a "Crisis," it doesn't really matter which one it is, the fact is they are going through Midlife "Something", hence "Woteva!"

Credits

Although most of what is written here are basically my thoughts and analyses, I have taken the liberty of including and adapting a deal from various sources. It is only right and proper of me to give credit where it is due. I have attempted to seek permission wherever possible. You might come across some of this information elsewhere. A lot of it is somewhere in the public domain and is frequently quoted and copied. The main websites I want to refer you to are www.

midlifecrisisforum.com, www.fortysixty.com, www.midlife.com, www. divorcebusting.com and www.coping.org. They are all free to join, and full of stories, hints and guides that will help you tremendously.

I apologise profusely for my adaptations or any seeming plagiarism. I thank and give credit to all the individual authors and contributors for a job well done. It was and is done with the best of intentions. There is also a lot of excellent and helpful information. I recommend you to research and read their papers and comments in full. I have tried to lead you to them wherever possible. To those of you who may have come across some of this before I say "Good," there is nothing like the reinforcement of great ideas. Others may be reading all of this for the first time. To you I say, "Even better." It may save you much time and effort. Please read as much as you can. It can and will help you. Everything might actually start to make sense!

Personal Note

I have to say that if I had known and understood all this information before (which there is no way I could possibly have expected to!) and implemented it to the letter (which I have to say now is rather like crying over "spilt milk!") I might have been able to better influence the outcome of my own relationship and saved myself, my partner, children, friends and family a lot of heartache.

"I love yo…. u, but I am **not** in love with you!"

CHAPTER 1

▼

INTRODUCTION

All marriages and relationships go through tough times. It has to be expected. We all think that we can take the rough with the smooth and that we will inevitably argue and make up. It's only natural, right? We can't agree on everything all the time, can we? We wouldn't be human, would we?

Saying that, even animals seem to disagree, be it over who gets the biggest bone or crust! But mostly we get over arguments, these hurdles that we encounter. We cool down, discuss things rationally and kiss, cuddle and make up. If only all of life was so easy!

There is a huge exception to the above however, and that is when one of us enters transition, most especially during the so-called period of life known as "Midlife." It is so confusing, seems absolutely impossible to deal with, and so infuriating, with no one to turn to for absolute answers, to offer a happy solution or a way out of the inevitable maze.

That is why I have written this book, to give an insight not only to my personal learning experience but also to those of hundreds if not thousands of others. You might get a clue, an understanding of what is happening to you and those around you. There are possible courses of action and strategies that ensure **you** look after yourself, and may help to save your relationship. After all, **you** are now the most important person in this seemingly impossible to deal with process.

If my father was writing this (sorry Dad), it would more than likely be a two-liner stating "Pull your socks up. Your partner doesn't want to be with you anymore, so get on with it! Why are you wasting your time writing or reading this stuff?" I am sure you have or will come across people like this. People you expected to understand, to be on your side and supportive. And yet, in truth, they do think they are helping, just not giving the type of assistance you were expecting or asking for. You were looking for answers, ways to make things right, not to get shot down in flames again, by those you thought were so close to you!

Now, for a word of warning! If you are looking for Freud or Jung, you have come to the wrong place. No "hi-falutin", mind bending exercises here. Not that these esteemed gentlemen are not brilliant in their own right, but because our journey to explanation will try to take the simplest and most direct route, regardless of the complexity of your situation as you may view it.

Many of the thoughts expressed here may be harmonious with their views, but this guide is for the average "Jack and Jill!" Do feel free to go away and read their theses, papers and complex or compounded views. They may well assist you in your search for answers, but I honestly hope and believe that what is included on the following pages may help do the same job for you, without the need to investigate the deep subconscious mind, expound theories, or make you ask too many more confusing questions. Strangely enough, although it may well seem quite complex to you now, the basis of MLC can be thought of in relatively simple terms.

You Are Not On Your Own!

LBS—You may have thought you were the only one going through this. You couldn't be more wrong. There are thousands of people just like you, hearing the same words every day. Some are in "Denial," others not brave enough to admit it or discuss it with family, friends or professionals. We all think that we have failed in some way and will be judged by others for it.

You may be surprised to learn that the same destructive statements or variations of them are made, repeatedly, all over the world, every day, in different languages! Believe me, you are far from alone!

Just in the knowledge that there really are many others, suffering as you are at this very moment, wanting to share their dark tales, success stories and help each other as much as possible will help you to get through this, not only to survive but also to thrive!

MLC—You too are not on your own. Remember that for every LBS'er by definition there has to be an MLC'er too! Many people going through "Transition" speak to and help each other on forums too. Don't hesitate to get involved or more information if you think it will help you.

Why Is This Not A Longer Book?

Trust me, you do not want or need a huge book for what you are going through at this time. We all want immediate answers to our problems, not having to trawl through 500 pages or 100 references to find things out. Like me, you might want something short and straight to the point that you can read or refer to over and over, something you can get through in one medium length sitting with a few cups of tea or coffee, if not something stronger. By the way, before I get shot down too quickly, alcohol is not the answer!

I know that I wanted quick answers and solutions. Maybe it is the same for you. If ever you want to know a secret, you might want to know it straight away, not having to find it hidden in a morass of other words. I trust you will not find this read a waste of time or money. Even if you find only one set of words of wisdom or a thought in these pages that you can act on, and I am sure you will find many, you will know both have been very well spent.

I am not attempting to preach to the converted, or the "unconverted" either for that matter. I am not intending to preach or lecture at all. Please do not take the book in totality or anything said in the following pages in that manner. It is all meant to be helpful, to give you at least a glimmer of hope in this matter of earthbound "hell."

Will I Find All The Answers Here?

The honest answer is probably not. A lot I trust, but probably not all. I have tried to address the core issues and be as comprehensive and concise as possible. I have included the major points that I think really need to be understood, digested and comprehended.

There are many other sources of information and professional help is available, but this relatively short read can help prepare you for a longer search. You may not need to. This may suffice for your reading matter. I do suggest that you read as much as possible or you are willing to, participate in Internet forums and discussions. They can and will help you greatly.

Will The Answers Given Really Apply To Me?

I cannot guarantee that all the answers given are absolutely correct or that they will apply directly to you or your situation. What I can say with confidence though is that I have managed to find some consolation and rationalisation in the explanations they provided to me and after discussion with many other people in the same situation I feel comfortable in offering them to you. After all, isn't it better to have a few reasonable answers than none at all?

How Is It Going To Be Presented?

It makes a lot of sense to break this book up into simple sections, following in sync with the course of the Midlife Transition or Crisis stages: Introduction, Before, Beginning, Middle, End and After The End, with Questions and Answers along the way and a few jokes to lighten up your journey. This way you might be able to identify which part of the process if any, you are now facing, and what to expect next.

Why Call It "The Kamikaze Experience?"

After experiencing the traumatic experience of partnership loss through Midlife as a "sufferer," I have now chosen to alternatively term it "The Kamikaze experience." Traditionally and internationally known as a "Midlife Crisis", I believe that we may be too polite at times. It simply is not a strong enough expression for it. It is like a huge bomb has hit us, delivered by our partner, destroying our little world with everything we lived for and believed in.

To us, our partners seem to be on a self-destructing mission. S/he has climbed into a nasty little plane and is determined to destroy the family boat below, her/his former life, containing family and friends, regardless of the consequences or how much damage is done. Some will parachute to safety, ditching the plane as they go, others not.

However, for sake of ease I will use the MLC reference throughout instead of constantly reverting between "Transition" and "Crisis." And yes, for you clever ones, I do know that Kamikaze pilots did not have parachutes! But ours are different, modern "Semi-Kamikazes" and we often run around wildly, trying to catch them as they fall and provide a soft or safe place to land!

Should I Let My Partner Read It?

In truth, there are two points of view. The first is definitely **not**. This information is primarily for you and only you. It gives you the basis of understanding, of methods to cope, and to reassure you that what you have heard is similar to or exactly the same as many others. It will help **you** prepare for the tricky way ahead.

The other point of view is that if your partner recognises that s/he is in MLC and wants to work through it and stay with you, you may want to and should offer all the assistance you can. And for this reason you may offer it to her/him. You have to be very careful though. The words, phrases and suggestions may only fuel the crisis even further. Worse than that, your partner may recognise how you are trying to cope with her/him. Your partner might try to appear to be very clever in this respect, making you feel foolish or even guilty for employing certain strategies in your attempt to cope with and save the situation.

You decide, if and when the time is right, whether to share what you know. **You** are now in control!

My Story

I was in a happy marriage, or so I thought, for 13 years before getting hit by the "bomb" of MLC. For a while I had a successful career, two lovely children and a beautiful and clever wife, who I adored. I never thought our marriage would ever be in jeopardy. I thought we were so strong as a couple and could survive anything that we might face forever more.

When I was young I imagined I could be a prince on a white horse, rescuing a damsel in distress, living happily ever after. At thirty-five I fulfilled that mission, even if only in my own mind. I rescued my damsel, living in what I believed were downtrodden circumstances with a young child. I imagined that she was my miserable princess, seeking rescue. I put her on a pedestal, built her up, encouraged her to establish her own position in life, to search her soul and find her hidden beauty, talent and confidence.

Unfortunately I became too complacent with our relationship and my master plan backfired on me. I had health problems and we struggled financially. I now also believe that I went through a transition period in my early forties. I didn't know then and only recognise that now. I freely acknowledge that I made life difficult for all of us. I was depressed and questioned what I was doing in life and my seemingly paltry achievements. I have overanalysed my part in all of this. I now believe that for a few years I was the "breadwinner" and my wife was the "homemaker." As time went on I failed to keep the balance and my wife took on more than her fair share of responsibilities. I can only describe this as her possibly having three children to contend with, although until recently I could not see it. I always imagined and hoped that by some miracle or "magic event" things would get better and the balance would be restored. However, at no time did I ever even think about leaving my wife, the marriage, having an affair or seeking solace elsewhere.

Instead of remaining with her self-professed "saviour" she found herself changing, that she was in flower, so to speak. She was able to address her earlier torment and failures, not happy with the way things had turned out and wanted to improve her life further, finding a real prince, not the surrogate that I had turned out to be in her eyes. And yet, although I now realise I did have faults, **this** situation was **not** my fault. There was **nothing** I could do to prevent, stop or avoid it.

Is A "Midlife Crisis" Really Responsible For What Is Happening?

LBS—You may have discussed "Midlife" with your partner who has told you in no uncertain terms that, regardless of what her/his mental state might be now or whether there has been or still is a "Crisis," s/he wants to do something different with life, and this may not include you. So whether an MLC is in progress or not is quite irrelevant at this stage. **You** need to deal with its effects on **you.**

MLC—You might think you are changing as a person or need to make changes to your life, to fulfil your destiny and ambitions. You know and acknowledge that others may be hurt in this process, but you want to be "true to yourself."

A Little More About Transitory Periods

We all change as we go through life. It is a very healthy process. We question what we have, what we want, and how we are going to get what we decide on. As discussed throughout this book we choose to categorise these periods individually e.g. Teenage, Midlife etc. These refer directly to our ages at the time. Just because we go through a transitory period does not mean we will create or participate in a "Crisis." During different transitory periods we may address different issues. During teenage years we might try to decide on our initial career or higher education path, our choice of girl/boyfriend, whether we want to learn to drive a car or motorcycle, where we would like to live etc. In our twenties we may decide whether we want to stay single, get married, have children, change careers etc. Later on, in Midlife we may decide to look again at the validity of any of these former choices, or other issues that have surfaced since that time, perhaps as a result of our former decisions.

So, just because we can say we are in a "Transitory period," that is no bad thing in itself. We may question, but be happy with the decisions we have made. However, during every "Transition" there is a risk that someone else may be hurt by our decisions or actions. It just so happens that in Midlife (when we are approximately half way through our lives) and we think that everything is settled, that any changes can have what seems like a more dramatic effect on our lives and those of everyone we know.

However, for the purposes of what we discuss here, we are focussing on what happens during those Midlife years.

When "Love" Is Not Enough

I really don't want to confuse you anymore than you may be already, but I think it is very important to emphasise that relationships break down for a number of reasons apart from Midlife Transition or Crisis. This might seem like an obvious statement, but I think that we (LBS'ers) may just jump at the first convenient "solution" without being able to think things through properly. That is why I have included the following:

It has been said that we are the sum of many things, and at the end of the day everything in life could be explained mathematically. There is a simplistic formula that can be applied to give a very simple summary of your position. **Your**

Net Worth (100%) = Personal Value (50%) + Extraneous Value (50%) So for example, let's say that you are a great person and score 40 in the first, but have little financial resources, so score 10 in the second. This gives you a total of 50. Money, or lack of it may have caused considerable stress in your relationship. So your (ex) partner has found someone else now. This person may score lower than you on the personal level, say 30, but has a job and money offering security (with another score of 30.) On the whole then, using this arbitrary scale, you may only score 50 versus the opposition at 60!

Your partner might say that money is not "the problem." It may not be the money directly in itself, more of what it can provide in terms of security, comfort, material possessions and treats! Do remember, money, however useful it may be, does not provide true happiness on its own.

But, you might say, this is rubbish, s/he was the breadwinner. This can't have been about money! My partner said s/he was never interested in money. I stayed at home doing other things, bringing up the family or, I was too sick to work. Remember that the above formula is not specific to money only. It was only used in the above as an example. All other aspects of your personality and relationship can form part of the extraneous part, e.g. sex, health, cooking, going out, having fun etc. You could do many calculations in a table, and total results up at the end.

Now, let's take this a step further. Let us assume that on initial analysis, you think you score the same as the OP (Other Person.) Well, haven't you forgotten something? The disagreements, the arguments, the problems however small they were that you shared together. The joint or singular "emotional baggage" that we all carry inside. I am afraid to say you can take some points away now from your own score! Of course, the OP has "baggage" too, but this has not been a shared experience with your partner, it will be slanted in her/his favour and can just be listened to, empathised and even sympathised with. Oh, if only they could hear the other side of the story, which they might well do, in time!

The fact that this might be happening at the same time or because of a Midlife "experience" does not help us get to a solution any quicker.

This indicates that a relationship consists of more than just "love." Other elements are equally important. Remember, these are only thoughts I am sharing with you. The above description is only a theory, a rule of thumb, and not to be taken too seriously. It is just one of many thoughts for **you** to consider!

Relationship "Crunch" Points

As mentioned, not all relationship problems are down to MLC, and people do change with time. This has to be recognised. Many experts agree that there are key stages to most relationships, and there are "crunch" times through which they will either survive or not.

The first period is "**Lust**." With few exceptions this only lasts a few months, during which time you and your partner can't keep your hands off each other. Many relationships end after the initial lustful period and a "pull" to another starts.

Second comes "**Attraction**," which lasts from eighteen months to three years. During this time you and your partner decide whether to stay together for longer or not, whether to get married, share your lives and/or have children together.

After this time, relationships have to rely more on general "**Compatibility**," where family and other jointly shared issues and interests keep you and your partner interested in each other.

You or your partner may start to look at others and find them attractive, but for the sake of your marriage and relationship make a conscious decision not to take things further.

In order to keep your relationship alive, the following are important:

- Expectations—even if you come from similar backgrounds, you may have different wishes, desires and ambitions. These need to be discussed and differences agreed between you.

- Communication is vital. You have to talk to each other, not "bottle" things up, discuss and resolve issues, and make plans together for the future. Look out for the difference in contact and communication that we discuss later. They are not the same.

- Appreciation of and for each other is very important. It is hard to sustain your feelings for your partner long-term, and it takes work to keep all relationships alive. You both need to appreciate each other, and keep reminding yourself and each other of your good points together.

When this happens not to be what you or your partner wants any longer, it might be time to think of moving on, with a desire to start the process again with someone new.

I am just trying to tell you that it might not be the effects of MLC you are experiencing. You might just not be "compatible" anymore, certainly in your partner's eyes. This must not be confused with MLC. You may just need to work very hard at relationship issues to resolve the situation, if you are both willing to.

Whose "Crisis" Is It Anyway?

Regardless of whether your partner thinks or agrees that s/he is going through MLC, you might think that **you** are going through a "Crisis." Your partner may well be in "Transition," only to seemingly think of her~/himself, not being able to make a decision in your favour, but what about you? Your life has been turned upside down. You don't know where to turn for help, what to do about any or everything, how you can possibly save your relationship. Anyone who says this is not a "Crisis" for you does **not** understand what you are going through.

I think this is such an important point to re-emphasise. S/he might be going through "Transition," but it is you who may be going through a "Crisis." Almost as if your partner is "happily" going through her/his MLT, but you can "suffer" or be "victimised" by the same person's MLC. This is not to say your partner will not experience a "Crisis" period of her/his own. Maybe s/he does, but it only comes to her/him when realising what has been done and try to address it. For the rest of the time, s/he is merely "Transitioning". It is all down to cause and effect!

When Does It Happen?

It is now generally accepted, although it is a rule of thumb that a "Crisis" of this nature can be created by both women and men anywhere between the ages of thirty-five to sixty. However, most reported Midlife Crises seem to begin at around the age of forty.

Alternatively, and maybe linked in some way, there are those that believe life happens in seven-year cycles. You must have heard about or experienced the so-called "seven year itch" in marriage? To take this a step further, there are major changes in our lives between the developmental years of childhood, the "teenage" years, the twenties, from thirty-five and forty-two, forty-two to forty-nine and so on. This theory also implies that these many developmental changes in life can take up to seven years to solidify, complete and play themselves out before the next cycle of life begins.

Just to confuse you a little more or maybe add a little credence to the timing, there are also those that believe that we have thirteen year life cycles. So we have might have these episodes at about thirteen, twenty six, **thirty-nine** and so on.

Whatever happens and whenever it does, you certainly need to be prepared for big and sometimes unexpected changes.

What Causes MLC To Happen In The First Place?

It would be extremely convenient and far too easy to give a very clear, doctor approved list of symptoms and causes, but that is not possible and would not be correct. What can be said with relative safety is that there are many similarities between one midlife crisis and another.

You will find that people say, "That's exactly what happened to me," "That's exactly what was said to me" and "That's exactly what s/he did!" There can be a lot of reasons, some put down to unresolved childhood or later age-related issues, a catalyst such as a recent or major life changing event, such as losing a parent or friend to illness, the feeling of getting old or "past it," not achieving what one thinks s/he ought to have at this stage of life, the children are growing up or leaving home or there may just be boredom with the day to day drudgery of life. You name it; it could bring on the onset of MLC. Even trying to cope with your own "Midlife" could trigger the start of your partner's "Transition." I now absolutely believe mine did! The list of causes is seemingly endless! Even though we all want to know why this happens, the fact is that we have to deal with it as best we can in our own way. We could spend forever looking for justification or the reasons why.

Somehow or other, a person going through "Transition" imagines and truly believes that s/he is now being given another chance in life. Time to reinvent her~/himself, to do things s/he wants and has never been able to, imagining that s/he is in teen years or twenties again with the benefit of experience and perhaps financial security. "Life is too short!" is often quoted. The long-term future doesn't matter anymore, just today and possibly tomorrow. Your partner feels a right to be selfish. "It is my time now, not anybody else's!" is often said. And guess what, we are the ones thrown into "Crisis!"

Is MLC Real Or Imaginary?

LBS—Let's cut to the chase here. This is **very** real, scarily real in fact. It is not an imaginary process that can be snapped out of, nor cured with drugs or hypnotism. It is a process that some if not all adults go through. Some cope far better than others. We all go through periods of transition during our lives (we have to grow up sometime.) Some will not put their family, friendships and their future at risk. Others throw caution to the wind, living life as never before. Some try something new and love it, or then decide it is not what they wanted after all. The grass looks so much greener on the other side of the fence, as is said, they just didn't choose to water their own instead!

MLC—As mentioned before, you might just think you are appreciating new things, changing old attitudes. This process is real, and may be causing problems for your partner.

Is MLC An Illness?

LBS—"But all I want is for her/him to get better" is often said by suffering LBS'ers (Left Behind Spouses.) There are two points of view. The first is that you should not regard MLC as an illness in a traditional medical sense. Your partner is not "sick." No drugs will cure her/him; they will only alleviate the symptoms. Your partner is undergoing a radical change to her/his personality, the core of her/his being, becoming a new person. Your partner will never get "better" as such. S/he will have altered. Your partner might behave differently, and seem to act in a "nice" manner later on again. It is a transition period for her/his mental state. It is a totally natural process in our personal growth and maturity.

The second very strong viewpoint is that aspects of MLC do display distinct symptoms of a "mental illness" at times. Your partner probably goes through a deep state of depression at some time which may last for a while, the rest of her/his life or until s/he gets professional help. Without aid the crisis might just be prolonged or masked with self-medication, putting "plasters" over deep wounds, hence having repeated affairs etc. looking for something, someone or answers that might not be found.

Failure to get help does not mean that the MLC will not end eventually on its own. If your partner does not choose to get help, which must only be sought because s/he wants to, it is highly likely that s/he will have a longer crisis than others do. Your partner might also never look at the issues or accept personal responsibility for what brought her/him into and out of it and what has been done.

MLC—You may not feel "ill" at all, just realise that what you have been doing is not what you want to do anymore.

<u>Anything I Can Do? I Want To Help!</u>

LBS—First of all remember that **you** are being seen as the "cause," the root of all the problems. You are viewed as the person with all the faults. How can s/he be expected to accept any help or advice from you? Also, you will be told many times over **not** to tell your partner that s/he is in Midlife Crisis. Your partner must discover this and deal with it her~/himself.

However, your partner may say that s/he does not know how s/he feels and might approach you, hinting that s/he is having difficulty with this or that feeling or situation. Your partner might be asking you in a round about way for help, but **not** for interference. This is when you could choose to assist in as gentle a way as possible without thinking that you are doing the wrong thing. Just don't try to do too much or too soon!

It might still be wise not to offer direct help. Remember your part in this and how you are being viewed. Your assistance might be seen as being done for selfish motives only and the immediate response could be to reject or purposefully ignore what you say. It could be more relevant and helpful to point her/him towards an independent third party, a professional counsellor, not necessarily a marriage counsellor but someone who can help her/him through this.

If your partner says that s/he might be in a Midlife Crisis without your prompting, then you may say that you have been reading up on it and refer her/him to a book, or a website where s/he can discuss her/his feelings with others. Let her/him do this freely, of her/his own will. You are both **not** alone!

MLC—You might not feel that you need any help to get through this. It is your personal situation that you are handling to the best of your ability.

Why Me, What Did I Do To Deserve This?

LBS—Hopefully, by the time you have finished reading partway into this book, you will realise that this is **not** about you at all, it merely affects you profoundly. It never has been and never will be. It is all to do with your partner. You probably did nothing really "wrong." You do not deserve to be treated like this, whatever you may think now. God or anyone else is not taking revenge for your past sins or mistakes.

Of course we all make mistakes, doing this or that wrongly along the way. Mostly, it must be said and in hindsight, with the best of intentions. That is how we learn and grow. In the normal course of events we forgive each other and carry on, making things better along the way. Midlife in whatever form is purely a personal life growing experience, and the losing partner unfortunately can just suffer the horrible fallout and consequences directly.

MLC—You may feel that your partner doesn't deserve this either. It is just unfortunate that s/he is around and may get hurt in the process.

What Should I Be Feeling?

The events that are happening to and around you are life-changing. Having been rejected, you might experience a great deal of stress. Be reassured that this is quite normal. You might show one or more signs of trauma. These include utter shock and disbelief, which may cause withdrawal from everyone and everything around you, feeling totally numb with pain.

You could seem to live in a dream world where nothing seems to be real anymore, you are just going about doing daily duties, then forgetting what you have done and having to go back and check. Everything may appear unreal to you, as if it isn't happening. You could experience anxiety related to the separation, thinking that this might have only been the tip of the iceberg, that more terrible things are about to happen. You may start to see images of your partner when he or she is not and cannot possibly be there, through simply wanting or wishing it to be the case.

You may be abusing yourself in some way, having turned the rejection against yourself in rage. You may have turned to smoking, pills, drugs, alcohol (or chocolate and ice cream) in an attempt to cope.

All of the above feelings are quite normal and should be expected in your situation. Don't try to deal with them alone. Get professional help as soon as you can!

What Are Some Other Symptoms I Might Experience?

You might withdraw sexually. As you try to preserve energy just to survive, you might shut down your reproductive side. Alternatively you may be sexually pro-active, attempting to prove that you are still attractive to one or the other sex.

You may lose weight. This is commonly known as the "MLC diet." In addition to not being hungry or enjoying food at the moment, you might feel that you need to lose weight to "win" your partner back. It must be said that some binge or "comfort eat" instead. Neither is particularly good for you, nor will they bring your partner back!

You might have trouble sleeping, or always wake up early. You may feel very anxious when you do. You may want to sleep constantly, just trying to escape everyday life and the situation.

You may appear to be washed out, miserable and depressed. This can be contributed to by a number of things including your continued loss of appetite, lack of sleep and improper exercise.

The above points again to the need that you have to look after yourself properly and get help if required. Start now if you haven't been doing so. No more excuses for inaction!

Why Do I Feel As If I Am Living In A Dream?

Your natural self-defence mechanisms are active now. You might feel that you are living in a dream. That everything is going on around you, but you are not part of it and can't participate properly. It could be that you are in a "trance" mode. This is where you retreat inside yourself, possibly to a childlike state, where you remain until you bring yourself out again.

We go into trances when someone says a word or a phrase that brings it on. It could be an event, being in a place or even a particular smell that brings back memories of an earlier time that we now feel the need to defend against.

This is totally natural, though it is a totally different and very interesting subject. You may wish to investigate trances and the child within you.

Why Do I Feel As If I Have "Died?"

You might feel that you are being treated as if you no longer exist. Your partner certainly seems to treat you as if you are no longer alive apart from the infrequent times you have contact, which might appear to be on a very indifferent basis. When you do see your partner, s/he seems to be getting on with her/his new life while you haven't or can't, still hanging on to the past with nowhere to go. This can be very upsetting for you.

The same scenario might apply with regard to aspects of communication. When your partner chooses to acknowledge your existence s/he might make contact, expecting a speedy and full response. However, when you try to call her/him or send an e-mail or letter, it is seen as unwelcome and your partner might not respond for days, if at all. When your partner does, answers might be very short, cold and to the point. Remember, you are no longer part of her/his life and will not be treated as such.

You may have withdrawn so much from everyone and life in general that you don't think you are part of this world anymore. You may be living the life of a virtual hermit, possibly for the first time. You certainly feel very alone.

You will have to accept that for the moment and foreseeable future you are no longer part of your partner's "new" life. Your partner has chosen to think that you don't even exist anymore, except when s/he has to. How else could your partner enjoy her~/himself now, with constant thoughts of you?

Just because your partner is now choosing to ignore you, you are not "dead," far from it. You need to start living life yourself again when **you** are ready, going out, seeing friends and family and making new contacts. You may be depressed and need to obtain medication from your doctor.

Remember, your partner is "dead" in a way too! Not physically, but in many other aspects. The person you once knew might look and sound the same, but s/he has changed. Her/his personality and thinking may have changed a lot. Your partner's attitude and feelings towards you certainly have. Your partner is no longer the one you loved so much. As hard as it is to accept, this may help you cope better with the situation.

Don't give up now; there is a lot of life left in **you**!

But S/He Is Not Being Nasty To Anyone Else!

LBS—Don't you believe it! It may not be in the same way as to you, but look out for the signs. There is a relatively simple answer to this. You have been the closest one to your partner. After all, you have shared everything to date. Imagine the parent/child relationship and how it may apply. Children and teenagers invariably react against the person/s that is/are closest to them. The one/s they feel safest with. The one/s they can rebel against and test their limits with. The one/s that love them unconditionally and will forgive their "naughtiness," in other words, their parents!

How many times have you thought your child or teenager was acting horribly, only for their friends' parents to say how lovely they were and wish theirs were the same? Think back to the time when you were growing up and how you behaved towards your parents. How you constantly tested their limits while developing yours. If you can think of what is happening in this way, you may begin to understand the whole situation just a little better. Of course, you may not accept this theory. Once again, it is up to **you**. Yet another personal choice!

In fact, your partner might be "horrible" to others as well. You just may not know it. Your partner might be ignoring, being rude to or dropping old friends and family members and expressing her/his inner anger at work colleagues too. Your partner might be difficult to live **and** work with. Your partner might be reserving her/his "happy" face for new contacts and friends, where s/he does not have to confront her/his hidden feelings and expose the truth.

Most MLC'ers are unhappy with their lives but don't really know why, certainly in the beginning. Your partner is looking for a reason for this unhappiness, the simpler the better, and to look inside her~/himself would be very painful. So your partner might rationalise in the following manner; s/he has been living with you for a long period and probably spent a lot of her/his waking and most of the sleeping time with you. Your partner seems to choose to remember that life was perfect before you came on the scene. Even the first years of your relationship may appear to be fine in retrospect. Therefore it must have been you who caused the damage and been the source of all this pain and anguish, making her/him unhappy (when it fact we know now that it wasn't!) Remember that pure and rational "logic" does not apply in MLC.

MLC—You might think that all you are doing is choosing your own "friends" more carefully, not wasting time with people you no longer agree or want to be associated with.

Why Is the Other Person So Different To Me?

LBS—If your partner is or has been having an affair you might wonder why the new person is so different to you and begin to believe all sorts of things about yourself and your failings. **Don't** do this! Remind yourself that this has nothing to do with you. It is all about them! Your partner is not happy with you or her~/himself at the moment. Your partner is now only in pursuit of personal happiness and satisfaction. Your partner might have believed at the time that you were wrong for her/him so the natural course of events would be to look at somebody as opposite as could be. This could be in terms of age, looks, personality or status, all four or more!

If that relationship does not work, in the course of time s/he might move on to another person. This one may be at the other end of the spectrum, maybe more similar to you. Strangely, this can be even harder for you to deal with!

Some choose basically the same type of person over and over. Your partner might be looking for the original you, the one s/he married all those years ago, and possibly repeat this activity ad infinitum, looking for "the one!"

In time, your partner may realise that what s/he was looking for was only the original you, the one s/he fell in love with in the first place! Remember, over the course of time you will have changed too, quite a lot during the period. There are no guarantees, but this may bring you together in the future.

MLC—You might think that your current/former partner is incompatible now and all you are trying to do is find someone that suits your new lifestyle and choices.

Why Is S/He Spending So Much Money?

There is no doubt that some MLC'ers seem to go on spending sprees, buying clothes, holidays, presents and goods with gay abandon. But why do they do it?

Sometimes it is just because your partner can and feels s/he deserves to do what s/he wants to for her~/himself. After all, in her/his mind s/he has been giving so much for years to everyone else. Some are trying to buy a new look to go with their transformation to a "younger" self, which may include new clothes, jewellery, household makeovers and even expensive surgery to try and buy back time and reinvent her~/himself. Your partner does not know or realise that this is a virtually impossible task!

The spending sprees might not relate to any of the products bought, but may actually be a process of your partner attempting to make her~/himself feel better, assuaging her/his conscience and proving independence.

Does S/He Experience Memory Loss?

So many times MLC'ers deny having said things to their partners when faced with the statements that may have been made. Maybe these comments were spur of the moment, not deeply held beliefs. Your partner might have been saying what s/he truly thought at the time or had been trying to say what s/he thought you wanted to hear. Your partner could have been attempting not to hurt you, maybe even to win you over to do something for yourself, or just to make you or her~/himself feel better about it!

At the same time, others say that they can't believe what the MLC'er has remembered. The smallest details of things are brought up from the past, even if yesterday's events can't be remembered! Some so trivial that even you needed to be reminded of them!

This can be very disconcerting. But remember, s/he is attempting to rewrite history and forget what s/he wants to about the past. Your partner is all in a muddle!

Do I Need To Apologise?

There is nothing wrong with apologising for something that you have done. Do it freely and mean every word of it, but only for what you can honestly state is your fault. Do not even attempt to apologise for something that someone else has done or is blaming you for, expecting you to take full responsibility for both cause and effect.

Very importantly, you need to forgive yourself completely for any of your faults or misbehaviours first. It is all very well to accept forgiveness from another but it is vital for you to become at one and happy with yourself, accepting that you have nothing to hide and that you are worthy of the greatest love and happiness too.

Understanding V Accepting And Forgiving

Don't assume or feel that you ever have to accept or condone bad behaviour from anyone. What we are attempting to do is understand what is going on and how to deal with it, to the best of our abilities. Understanding, rationalising and trying to explain these behaviours leads to eventual healing. Accepting and forgiving what has happened and is happening requires a totally different set of skills.

Will S/he Ever Come Out Of This?

Most do, eventually. But not overnight. It can take what seems like a very long time. MLC'ers don't snap out of this! Your partner will work or process her/his way through the many stages. These are detailed in depth later on. Sometimes s/he re-enters what you might have thought were stages that had long been exited. Unfortunately, I can't guarantee that all will emerge from the MLC into happy second adulthood. Some remain unhappy with life for a very long time.

Some will never have the ultimate courage to face their demons and continue to replay their fantasy life for some time. However, there is good news. Most do come out of MLC and continue to lead happy and fulfilling lives. Some stay with, or get together with their former partners; others do not. Either way, s/he really will be a further developed human being, having gained a far greater knowledge about her~/himself, including motivations and limitations.

It must be stated that your partner might not be a "better" human being after this process either, just a different one!

How Long Does It Last?

There is no definite time period for a Midlife Crisis. However, it is generally accepted that an average of five years is to be expected from beginning to end. Some complete the course of the "Transition" in a shorter period, and there are reported cases on the other side of seven to ten years. Most do and should be expected to complete in the average of five years though, though seven would tie in nicely with the theory of life cycles.

Will S/He Ever Be The Same Again?

No! Both you and your partner will not be the same as you were before the "Transition" or "Crisis." Don't fall into the trap of thinking that things will ever be "back to normal" again. Your partner cannot and will not be. Both of you will have changed in some major respects, in attitudes and behaviour patterns. Some aspects of each will be similar to the original characters, with minor tweaks. Other changes may be quite radical. Your partner may seem to be better or worse in your opinion!

It could be that you do choose to get together again in the future. Your earlier relationship will and must always be confined to the past. Of course you will retain the memories of before, hopefully only the good and happy ones will rise to the surface. If you choose to, you may develop an even stronger love for each other. You will have to set and agree new rules and boundaries about many things. You may be able to forgive but never truly forget what you have been through. One of your challenges will be not to bring up these painful memories, over and over again, or use them as a weapon against your partner in the future.

It takes a lot of work to rebuild a relationship between two formerly (or formally i.e. divorced) estranged people. It is easier sometimes to start again with someone completely new! Trust and commitment have to be paramount in any close relationship. If you choose to go down this path, both of you will need to be prepared to work extremely hard to make a success of it.

Will There Be Any Regrets?

I strongly believe from what I have read and learned that there will be regrets at some time in the future, when the storm has passed and the MLC'er can see what has been done. We all do have a conscience, however well hidden or disguised it may seem to be. Some more than others though, it must be said! Some will never have or show regret for what they have done, saying that it was just one of life's lessons and experiences.

How often have you heard the story of someone coming back on bended knee, begging for forgiveness, or is this just in fairy stories? Please don't be fooled for a minute. This will and does not happen in all cases. Some are genuinely happy with their new lives, and do wonder why they didn't make a move earlier. Many are not. They are so consumed with guilt that they feel they cannot return, are not prepared to face the consequences and will never admit they were wrong, as much as they would like to. There are stories of individuals who only seem to face up to what they have done on their death beds, begging forgiveness at this last stage of their lives.

Hopefully, when you finish this book, you may find hope within yourself too that this is not the end, but the beginning of your new adventure. After all, you have half or more of your life left, don't waste it!

Why Don't I Feel Like Doing Anything?

From talking to many others we agree that our energy levels are directly linked to our emotions. When we feel sad we don't want to do anything, just to hide from the world, feel sorry for ourselves and wallow in our misery. But when we feel angry, we somehow seem to find the energy to do anything and everything. Of course, when we feel normal and well balanced, we just get on with things!

It is almost as if we give our energy subconsciously to our partners or the situation at our own expense. We do have to think and act so carefully all the time not to upset the applecart!

This may explain why you feel quite apathetic at times and seem to have that seeming lack of energy to do anything yourself.

That is also why, as soon as you start to feel happy with yourself again, you will feel like doing so much more.

How Can I Stop Thinking About This? It Hurts So Much!

You might find it virtually impossible to think about anything else at the moment, however hard you attempt to. Try the following. The objective of this exercise is to focus your mind on things that are external to you and escape from all those internal nagging thoughts. What you can do is this; go to a quiet place, sit or lie down, relax and just listen to everything you can hear. For example, the sound of traffic passing, birds, the wind, and the buzz of the computer etc. Also, experience your clothing and how it feels against various parts of your body. Focus really hard on these thoughts and nothing else. Try hard to listen for everything that you possibly can and shut every other thought out.

By doing this, you are making yourself appreciate what is happening right now. All that is around and not inside you. It can provide you with some temporary relief from the stress of those thoughts that are bothering you.

You may need to practise this a lot. As you know, practice makes perfect. You will need to learn to dismiss those internal, harmful thoughts, as and when they pop up during this time.

If you find this helpful, do this is often as you wish to!

Why Can't I Sleep Properly?

You may be finding it difficult to get to or remain asleep, waking up at all hours. There is a good reason for this. Your mind is in turmoil. During the day you possibly have many things to do, but at night all you have is your thoughts, perhaps some that you have managed to put to one side. All these may surface in your quieter moments. You process a lot of your inner thoughts at night when you are not distracted and your mind tries to make sense of them. These are reflected in dreams or nightmares and their interpretation. If you can't sleep, get up, have a break, then try again.

You may wish to take something to aid your sleep, either a homoeopathic or traditional medicine to help you. Try orange juice or a hot milky drink. Proper exercise, relaxing CDs and hypnotherapy programmes may assist too. Please note that alcohol may help you get to sleep and dull the pain initially, but it will not help you get a good night's rest.

So Why Do I Want To Sleep All The Time?

You might be mentally exhausted, anxious or depressed and want to rest. When you go to sleep you can leave the reality of your situation behind temporarily, escaping into the world of dreams and desires for hours on end. It is possibly the only real peace you can find at the moment. This is how you have coped since childhood and the pattern is ingrained into your subconscious. Also, when you are asleep you believe that no one else can disturb you. You don't have to talk to anyone or explain yourself. Perhaps this is why you just want to go to sleep as much as possible, even if you have difficulty getting to sleep when you do go to bed. On the other hand, you may just be very tired!

Interestingly, MLC'ers also seem to want to sleep a lot. This is a form of escape from reality for them too. You may both look forward to this resting time to think on your own without disturbance to make decisions, formulate plans and strategies for the future.

Whatever the case, if you are not sleeping normally, seek the advice of your doctor.

How To Deal With—S/He Makes Me Feel So….

So many people say, "But s/he makes me feel so …" This is not what does or should happen in reality. Think of it this way; if someone you are not interested in says s/he loves you and you don't feel anything for her/him, you don't automatically feel that love in return. In fact you probably feel nothing at all. You are in control of your emotions in that situation. Therefore, when your partner says something to you, it is always your choice to accept, interpret and visualize what has been said that makes you feel happy or sad. You have a choice of accepting that thought and taking it on board. No one else can make you happy, sad or experience any other emotion; you allow it to affect you! Believe it. Think about it. It's true!

If It Is To Be, It Is Up To Me!

This statement is so true. It is how you handle the crisis that will determine **your** future. You need to decide what **you** want to do. Whether you are willing to ride it out. Deciding if and when **you** have had enough. What **you** are going to do? There is no guarantee that you will be together in the future. Can **you** manage to live like this for five years or so? It is all a question of what **you** want now and for the future of **your** life.

What Is MLC, Is It Real?

So what is a "Midlife Crisis?" Is it real? Is it as bad as people make out or just an excuse for bad behaviour? As sorry as I am to tell you, I have to have to reveal that

it is very real. It **is** as bad or seemingly worse than people make it out to be, and although there are no excuses, it can provide the reason for bad behaviour.

That is not to say that many people do not confuse or use MLC as an excuse for what is happening to them or their partners, but in many cases this is a very real experience. It certainly feels like it to those of us caught up in it.

It is a period of life where individuals question their self-worth, their current status, past failures and future plans. You can look at it another way, by breaking life into a number of stages. Infancy, early childhood, teenage years, twenties and thirties, forties and fifties (Midlife) and the years thereafter too unkindly known as retirement or old-age. Forgive me for this, you may be in the older age group and still quite rightly believe you are young at heart!

The Midlife transition period has been most closely linked in similarity to the teenage one, where we made most major life decisions. Feelings can be related to teenage angst and this may be why many MLC'ers say that they feel like a teenager again! Just remember how much you dreamed about what you were going to be, changing your mind and plans throughout those years! Also what you did, if you are not too ashamed to admit it! Well, think of an MLC'er as possessing a "teenage" mind in an adult body. It is much the same.

For those of you in the first throws of it all, it may help to have a definitive course of this so-called "disease." Although many people in MLC will go through the phases for different lengths of time, and in a different order, we have a description later on of what they may be going through, what they might be feeling and how long it takes.

Why Am I Putting Myself Through This?

It is important to remember your marriage vows when you consider why you are thinking about this and are seemingly prepared to put up with so much. Regardless of what your partner says or thinks now, you probably still take those vows very seriously; to honour and obey, through sickness and in health, for richer or poorer, until death do you part. At the time of your wedding you both meant every word. **You** might still do. **You** are trying to maintain your original faith and promises. You knew you would have to work on your marriage to keep it alive. That it would not all be easy.

How Will I Know When It's Over?

This may be a strange question to try and provide an answer to so early on, but we all want to know this, as quickly as possible. I know it was one of the most important questions I was asking, over and over, to anyone who would listen, and to many who wouldn't. No one could or would give me a definite answer. That is, except my partner, who had a definite answer for everything!

The simple answer is, somehow or other you will know when it is. Either your relationship will truly be over, you will have had enough and be either considering or have made your mind up to divorce, or your partner will have come to you, apologising profusely, showing true respect, commitment and a will to work things out, with nothing to hide anymore, no hiding or secrets, for all the harm and damage done to you, your relationship and others that **will** have been affected.

As long as s/he wants to keep some or all of this life a secret from you, the MLC is not truly over. Your partner is not ready to commit **fully** to your relationship, **or** any other, for that matter!

How Long Will It Take Me To Get Over This?

This is an excellent question and one that deserves the best answer money can buy! Another rule of thumb for you, and this guidance comes from sources dealing with the death of a loved one. The reason for this is that it is the most closely related experience to MLC that we will probably ever go through. It is said that if you allow one month for every year that you spent together, this would probably be a good guide. So, if you were with your loved one for a total of twelve years, it could around take around twelve months to realise what is happening, get over the shock, not to grieve anymore, and start living properly again.

This does not mean you will not retain memories, but you will feel able to act again, to do things on your own, without feeling guilty. You may feel that you have allowed enough time for your partner to make amends, without prejudicing the outcome. **You** will have earned your freedom too, be it the hard way!

Separate The Person From The Action!

You might ask, "How can it be that I love and hate her/him at the same time?"

A good method of coping with this is to separate the whole situation from the individual, the actions from the person. It is quite possible to love someone, but not to like or approve of something that s/he is doing. Just think back to the parent-child relationship. If your child does something naughty, does it mean you love her or him any less? You may not approve of the actions, but you will try to be there to help and see her/him through it.

By separating the two, you will find it easier to cope with these mixed feelings.

Setting Boundaries

It is vitally important for you to set personal boundaries, and to communicate those to your partner. This might be very early on in the crisis or you may choose your own time to implement them, when **you** are ready. This could include the fact that you will not be spoken to disrespectfully, that your personal business is only to be discussed between the two of you, not with others and that the children are not to be used as pawns in negotiations etc.

Perhaps the best way to illustrate this concept is in the form of a message:

"You know that I love you. This I will continue to do. Not because I have to, but because I desire to. This is possible because I have separated your person from your actions. Please take the following in the most amicable way. I mean no harm or disrespect. Quite the opposite! I just have to set ground rules for my expectations.

From now on I will afford your actions or lack of them with equal respect. This goes for requests too.

You are not acting as a friend and have deliberately chosen not to do so. Actions may well speak louder than words. When and if you choose to offer this to me, I will gladly become as close a friend as you wish to be. This goes for everything else. From now on please only expect to get what you are prepared to give in return in equal measure.

Your lifelong friend, if you so wish."

Of course, your message will be different; perhaps citing specific instances or examples of behaviour that you do not find acceptable. What this will do however, is make your partner think things through carefully from now on before communicating and stop her or him continuing to treat you with total "indifference." Just be careful what you write. Think about every word before you commit it to paper.

The other question that might arise is "When should I do this?" As suggested before, implement this as soon as possible. You will not be forcing the course of the MLC ahead. All you will be doing is showing your intelligence, maturity, personal strength and unwillingness to accept cruel or inappropriate behaviour.

This does not need to be done all at once. Each time that something else comes up, you might phrase a similar statement, mentioning what is on your mind. Don't save it all up and let a great volley off at once. There may be too much to take in, absorb and act on. Keep a note of it all for future reference somewhere private, and be careful, you might find you have enough material to write another book!

Finally, it is also very important that you stick to your boundaries. If they turn out to be "empty threats" they could well have the opposite effect and encourage the behaviour to continue or expand and show that you are still the weak person s/he thought you were. And remember, you are not setting the boundaries just for your partner. You are doing this for yourself, your sanity and **your** future!

"We will love each other **forever** and ever, right?"

CHAPTER 2

▼

BEFORE (THE HAPPY YEARS?)

This is a really short chapter, a "two-pager," as this is not the direct subject of our discussion. You can probably write your own. We will dispense with it in a few words. This was a time when everything was fine, normal and what we expected. Nice romance, great wedding, happy marriage, children, good career etc. Of course, we all had a few disagreements, not necessarily arguments, we had to, and it was expected. Establishing the rules, getting used to living with another, deciding who was going to be the disciplinarian etc. To explain this further; Who cooks the meals? Who does the decorating? Who cuts the grass? Who does school visits? Who tells the kids off if they have done something wrong or have been naughty? These may have been the source of many control issues, all the aspects of normal married life that were to be expected.

I will ask you to do a little work now. Here are a few questions that you can answer yourself before we really get into the "whys" and "wherefores." They will help you prepare for the questions you will be asked by others and possibly those you are asking yourself. Some are more difficult than others, and may take some time to think about.

- How long have you known your partner?

- How long did you romance each other?
- How long was it before you got engaged?
- Is this your first marriage or long-term relationship?
- How long was it before you got married?
- How long have you been married?
- Do you have any children?
- Have either of you experienced a life-changing event recently, either to yourselves, your family or friends?
- Had you noticed anything was wrong?
- Is there another person involved?
- Is this the first and only time?
- Have you always argued?
- Have you noticed different behaviour patterns?
- Do you think you are at fault?
- Do you willingly accept responsibility for your actions?
- Are you prepared to apologise for your own faults?
- Have you forgiven yourself?
- Are you prepared to forgive your partner?
- Are you prepared to put the past behind you?

"It's all **your** fault, not mine!"

CHAPTER 3

▼

THE BEGINNING (IS THERE A STORM ON THE HORIZON?)

I have to clarify what I am calling the beginning. You might not be aware of the actual start date, I certainly wasn't. The crisis often begins without any of us knowing about it. It wasn't a "crisis" then. It starts with a state of general dissatisfaction in the air. Not a lot, not about anything important. But two things come up. Then three and so it goes on. Eventually the straw comes along that breaks the camel's back. It is too much to bear, and an all-out war on life or you breaks out.

It was not until our personal "Crisis" was in full flow that I became aware of what was happening, and then I was too late to stop it. Interesting to think that I even thought I had any ability to stop any of this. I couldn't have, no one can or should think they have the power to. You cannot shake someone out of Midlife Crisis or give her/him a medicinal remedy. It is impossible to, has a power of its own and should not be halted mid-stream. It needs to resolve itself.

This does not mean that we either have to condone or agree with it or what people do during the course of MLC. I just mean to say that it happens and we have to live through and past it to the best of our ability.

Everything seemed to be going so smoothly, maybe with a few little "bumps." Then all of a sudden life hits. There may have been a few disagreements, arguments or silences. Things don't seem like they used to be. One or the other starts to go out on her/his own. Your partner starts doing different things. Your partner starts siphoning off money, spending, drinking, drug taking, partying, buying motorbikes, sports cars, jewellery, clothes, personal presents and bigger televisions. All of these individually do not necessarily mean that there is a Midlife Crisis in progress, but they are indicators to be closely aware of.

A relative dies, someone close has a critical illness, one of you loses your job or kids are growing up and leaving home. All of these examples make an individual start questioning her/his mortality, self-worth, place in society and achievements to date. Whether your partner has what s/he feels deserving of and set out to do in early adult life. Some live in acceptance of these events, others do not. Your partner thinks that every aspect of life should now be evaluated and perhaps start over again, with the benefit of experience. After all, it's never too late, is it? That's certainly what my dad used to say, and even my closest friends tell me now!

An MLC Test

I have adapted and included the following self-test from midlife.com to allow you to see if you or your partner may be experiencing a Midlife Transition or Crisis. This is not a "definitive" test. It is only an indicator. However, it is very important to state that just because you may tick a few boxes does not mean that there is a "Crisis" in progress. It is quite normal to question things and make changes in your life. This could just be termed "growing" in some way and could be termed "healthy transition."

Please be very careful with your interpretation of the results. At the same time, you may wish to complete this exercise in total privacy on behalf of your partner as you see her/him now. It may guide you to see the level of Midlife s/he is in. Be warned however; do not share your conclusions with your partner. They might deny all or some of it. It could be the cause of huge, unnecessary arguments.

The following may help you to understand if you or your partner may be experiencing a "Transition" and then to determine how severe this might be.

Tick each question that applies to you or your partner and at the end add them up.

Do you or your partner:

Question	You/Partner
Often think about running away	___/___
Find it hard to make decisions	___/___
Get frustrated as so much is spent on others	___/___
Drink, smoke, or take drugs	___/___
Get bored with your old friends	___/___
Want to make new friends, who don't know your history	___/___
Get angry easily	___/___
Not trust anyone you know	___/___
Increasingly forget things	___/___
Feel frequently depressed	___/___
Feel angry that everyone else comes first	___/___
Feel more irritable and nervous	___/___
Feel less sexually interested in your partner	___/___
Constantly criticize your partner	___/___
Feel useless or inadequate	___/___
Think that your body is out of shape	___/___
Want to have an affair	___/___
Feel that you have lost your faith	___/___
Want your youth back	___/___

Work out, as a new hobby	___/____
Want a new wardrobe or new look	___/____
Have reduced satisfaction with your job or career	___/____
Want to end it all	___/____
Total	___/____

Remember that the above is just a guide only, that is all. We all question aspects of our lives and achievements, continually and repeatedly as we wander on our paths.

If you checked 1 to 5 boxes, this can show some signs of perhaps starting or being in a Transition. Focus on understanding what these are and then how they can be handled, so that you do not have to face potentially tragic experiences unnecessarily.

If you checked 6 to 11 boxes, this could be the centre of a Transition. There is hope as you learn extensively about Midlife, get involved in counselling, work toward increased marital satisfaction and interpersonal relationships and try to improve your job situation.

If you checked 12 boxes or more, then there is probably a Midlife Transition in progress, which may be causing you a lot of stress and pain. But don't give up! Commit to learning as much as you can to understand the elements of a Midlife Crisis. It is crucial to understand your feelings of loss and to get help.

Remember, it is only when the effects of the "Transition" uproots your life that it may become a "Crisis" that you have to deal with in the best way you can.

"I have a present for you, **look out!**"

CHAPTER 4

▼

MIDDLE (THE CRISIS)

For the purpose set out at the start, the "middle" will refer to the passage of the "Crisis" itself. This is by necessity the longest section of our book. We will start by looking at what a Midlife Crisis is, i.e. seeing what we were, what we are and what we think we want to become.

We will start by looking at the process of a classic MLC. This has been adapted from a personal posting on midlifecrisis.org, but it has been altered and published on many other sites too.

Please, let me remind you to beware that this is a guide only. Times and stages may vary greatly, not only in their complexity but also in their order. Some may even occur together.

Stages Of MLC—A "Classic" Approach

1st Stage of a Midlife Crisis (Timeline Guide Year 1)

Denial

The word denial should speak for itself, as a person in this stage denies her/his feelings pretty strongly. In a Midlife Crisis however, there are several things that are denied; one is the fact s/he really is getting older, with a body that either doesn't work as well or look as good as it used to. Your partner feels "used up" but isn't even trying to fight that feeling. Your partner doesn't want to face the fact s/he is "wearing out" and can't do some of the things s/he used to do anymore. Your partner had always, up to this point, felt that s/he was still in the prime of life or youthful, and was ignoring the aging that was sneaking up.

When it finally hits home, s/he panics and may consider using plastic surgery to enhance the illusion or going on a buying spree for new clothes that don't exactly fit someone of her/his age. Your partner usually ends up spending a great deal of money on other things. All in an effort to "buy-off" the aging process—it only leads to the next stage—Anger.

Your partner looks at the children, and in her/his mind's eye, they are still small, never mind they are now teenagers that are on the verge of growing into adulthood, attempting to treat the young men or women as they did when they were three or four years old. The teens are probably about 13 to 18 now and start to rebel against being treated like small children. Alternatively they might be treated as adults now, taking your former place in some way. They are not prepared for this either. This increases the confusion of the "Midlifer"—s/he goes on to try and make up for lost time, only to find rejection at the hands of her/his teenagers, and though s/he may be hurt, can react in the only way s/he knows how—Anger.

Then there is you, the spouse of the "Midlifer"—you don't look the same as you did. As your partner ages, so do you, and we cannot help what heredity does to our looks; but you are a reflection of her/him, how s/he has treated you, what has been given or withheld, and s/he begins to deny what is being seen, thinking if s/he had it to go all over again s/he might have married someone else and been happier than now—never mind that it's not true—and that leads to the same stage—Anger.

Denial is mostly quiet storming inside one's head. No one knows what s/he is thinking, only that s/he has become withdrawn somewhat because of an overactive mind, and not talking, so no one has any clue what's happening until the Anger stage begins. If asked, your partner will tell you s/he is fine, and if you listen closely, answers are a little short-tempered, because s/he just wants to be left alone to think it all out.

It could take as short as a month or as long as six months to play out this stage.

Being unhappy within her/his job has not been included in the stage of Denial, because it is believed that dissatisfaction with a job does not really begin until the Anger stage. To be totally honest, we don't see our partner's dissatisfaction with this aspect of life and really come to the surface until the tail end of Replay, although it may show while s/he is in Replay—in small spurts.

2nd Stage of a Midlife Crisis

Anger (Timeline Guide Year 2)

While the "Midlifer" is in the Denial stage, it is actually preparing her/him for this next stage, it seems be a "set up" or the seeds of Anger are actually planted by being in that first stage. Regardless, Anger begins to set in, reality hits somewhat and the "Midlifer" begins to be really angry with the "lot" s/he has been cast in this life. Your partner has a tendency to forget that others have the same problems—s/he begins to be selfish, lashing out verbally at others, not caring how much it hurts the people that are closest, even at her/his boss, not caring if s/he loses her/his job. It does not matter to her/him, and s/he really can't explain the Anger. The irritability alone wears on her/him resulting in more anger—not really understanding the reasons for it, but just going on with it, thinking that s/he is saying what is really felt for the first time in her/his life, walking all over and using or abusing anyone who stands in the way.

Your partner might begin to think "run-away" thoughts, angry at the perception that s/he is "stuck" in the same dead-end job, year after year, angry that your children have grown up without her/him, angry that you aren't what s/he think you ought to be, angry that life has dealt her/him such a cruel blow, angry because s/he feels "stuck" and "trapped" in the life path chosen in youth. Angry because it dawns on her/him that s/he is growing older, and there really is no stopping the aging process.

Your partner begins to think if only s/he could just change her/his life, s/he would be happy, but even the thought of having to change makes her/him angrier. Your partner looks for outside sources to blame for this unhappiness that s/he feels inside, and guess who gets the "brunt" of that anger—you, the wife/husband of course—the one who has seen her/him through many things during the marriage.

Her/his Anger takes the form of small criticisms to begin with and gradually gets bigger and bigger and fights escalate into possibly throwing things against the walls, perhaps making impossible demands—you might begin to walk on "eggshells"—the withdrawal gets worse, couples can barely speak to one another without a fight breaking out from you, the affected spouse, trying to say or do the right thing which inevitably becomes wrong.

It begins to feed her/his justification and reasoning, and most will find a "friend" and develop that friendship, never dreaming it will escalate into something out of control—the "Replay Affair." Others might begin to take drugs, drink, continue with their quest for youth, and search of self … etc.

So to the next stage—Replay, which overlaps Anger, just as Denial and Anger did—each one has elements of the next and one before.

And all of these angry outbursts gradually set things up for the next stage—Replay.

The Anger stage can last anywhere from three to nine months.

3rd Stage of a Midlife Crisis

Replay (Timeline Guide Year 3)

Replay can take many forms, from multiple affairs to a search for youth, catching up on "lost" time—although you can never "catch up" with what has been lost in that time—but s/he doesn't know or realise that yet.

Your partner is still searching for outside sources to blame for her/his misery, and Replay is a perfect time for a totally stable man or woman to go "crazy" and start an affair—although the seeds for this affair were probably planted while in the Anger stage. Your partner will still try to reconnect with the children, or if they were close, distance from them. It is also during this time s/he becomes the total "opposite" of what s/he was before entering the tunnel, back in Denial. Your partner undergoes a gradual change in the first two stages, going from what was to what seems to be a direct opposite during this time. Your partner probably will do things you never thought s/he would do.

Besides the affair/s, your partner will feel "entitled" to take whatever s/he can, regardless of who is hurt or how much of a financial bind s/he puts her~/himself or the family in. Her/his reasoning becomes "Well, I have taken care of other people my whole life, now it's time for **me** to have **my** fun."

Emotions during this time are in play in a way they never have been, and s/he doesn't understand what's going on, so panics and "runs" but the running will rock the very foundations of the marriage.

Your partner may drink, smoke, take drugs, curse God for what he "has done" to her/him and have multiple affairs, failing to see what is being done that's so wrong—still with the attitude of it being "my" time now.

The "bomb" can and will be dropped during this time, shocking you who probably had no idea that anything was wrong, and problems begin to escalate. As "crying and begging" ensues, the "Midlifer" turns away, secure in her/his "reasoning" for any behaviour and/or the affair/drinking/drugs/money spent.

This behaviour can disrupt the most settled of families, most especially the affair/s. The "Midlifer's" reasoning is that s/he thinks s/he has "missed out" when in reality s/he hasn't. The other women or men (OW/OM) s/he can/does get involved with will not be what was wanted all along. Your partner won't see that until s/he experiences an "Awakening" that gives her/him direction and starts her/him along the path to facing her/his issues; opening the door for the stage of Depression.

As long as the "Midlifer" continues "Replay" behaviours s/he is nowhere near to being ready to start out of the tunnel; the "Awakening" experienced if and when s/he comes to it, is a "turning point" to beginning the journey out of the tunnel.

When the "Awakening" occurs, s/he begins to suffer the next stage—Depression, and it is a true low point in the "Midlifer's" journey.

The Replay stage is the longest of the stages and can last up to two years or longer, depending on the "Replay" behaviours used during this time.

4th Stage of a Midlife Crisis

Depression (Timeline Guide Year 4)

We have now travelled through the first three stages. To date, the issues that are inside the "Midlifer" have still not been looked at or addressed by her/him properly.

Depression is when the "Midlifer" faces the issues s/he can identify, and quite frankly, feels like a failure.

Nothing has helped in the first stages—everything s/he has tried has not turned to gold. On the contrary, everything may have turned to "stone" for lack of a better word, to describe her/his running. Now comes the time to begin to face the damage, and this is done inside, because that is what depression is, anger turned inward.

Your partner's hormones are probably out of whack due to physical changes, and that makes her/him feel worse. Your partner's self-esteem is shot to pieces, and s/he feels like a failure. Your partner wonders if s/he will ever be worth anything to anyone. Some are in so much pain they commit suicide. Your partner may get help and take anti-depressants to help them begin to clear her/his thinking process. Your partner may suffer through this in silence, thinking that nobody understands her/him or what s/he is going through—and so it carries on.

Your partner may be on the verge of tears much of the time, pacing the floor, losing sleep, afraid of the dark or maybe what's in it; unable to escape negative thoughts, cutting her~/himself down in word and action. Extreme guilt may compound this stage, and there is so much pressure, s/he becomes forgetful, irritable, wants to be left alone, becomes somewhat argumentative and sometimes unresponsive. Your partner wants to take long drives, walks or bike rides, sitting looking out the window or on a bench somewhere, lost in thought. Her/his silences are long and painful, as s/he doesn't want to talk, preferring instead to think and brood.

You must understand that s/he will either come through this or not. No one can "make" her/him come out until ready. Pestering your partner only makes her/him draw inside further. Your partner needs space to work within her~/himself, trying to understand some of what has happened. The parts that s/he can face, anyway, besides resolving issues that are deep inside, from childhood and/or later. Understand, also, this journey must continue to made alone, no one can "fix it" or "do it" for her/him.

Pieces of the next stage are contained within and Withdrawal begins to come to the fore as each individual issue is faced. The slide from Depression to Withdrawal can be gradual or both stages can occur simultaneously.

Depression can last from around two and a half to possibly six months, depending upon the severity your partner is suffering.

5th Stage of a Midlife Crisis

Withdrawal (Timeline Guide Year 5)

The "Midlifer" has begun to face her/his issues while in Depression, and what s/he has seen has not been pretty. Your partner has done so much damage. Your partner really doesn't know how to "fix" it, which has made her/him feel even more depressed.

So, for a time, your partner concludes that life is not worth much, and so "drops out" of life or withdraws, hence the stage of Withdrawal.

It is also during this time, s/he will navigate obstacles and question her~/himself, somewhat, working her/his way towards what is called the "Final fears." Not much is known about what final fears contain. Maybe it is beginning to accept the death of everything s/he has ever known, including that of her/his "old" life. Beginning to accept her/his own mortality without being afraid of it. Depression sets your partner up for this journey across an open field towards an "Archway" to face these fears. During this time, your partner will not communicate with anyone, especially you, as s/he is drawn so far within no one can reach her/him. Your partner must be allowed to continue, with no interruptions, just as before. Your partner will not come out until ready to emerge.

As in Depression your partner wants to be left alone, processing issues and the damage s/he has done to you, the family and her/his life. Your partner may make several decisions during this time concerning her/his life, job and marriage, but these won't be known until s/he breaks Withdrawal and really talks to you for the first time.

Your partner is still secretive, somewhat asserting her/his privacy, much like a teenager, but during this time must be gently but firmly led along. This must be done only when the time is right. Even the right words at the wrong time will cause her/him to "stick" within the tunnel.

You will see some Depression and Anger within her/him. Your partner is mostly angry with her~/himself, but will take it out on you, the LBS'er. There are times you will have to be quiet and just leave her/him alone. Let your partner work things out, and s/he usually will. The answers will come from within, not from outside sources.

As your partner begins to come forward, s/he will begin the journey out of the tunnel, entering the first stage of Acceptance.

Withdrawal can last from three months to one year.

6th Stage of a Midlife Crisis

Acceptance (Timeline Guide Year 5 to 6)

The "Midlifer" has navigated through five stages of her/his crisis by now, and begins venturing into final stages of Acceptance.

Acceptance is entered in three "Stages."

Stage ONE involves the disintegration of her/his personality. The "veil" is lifted showing the "Midlifer" everything, no holds barred. Your partner realizes for the first time just how much damage has been done to the marriage, her/his life and to you. You will be surprised to see elements of "children" surface, as well as "flashes" of the "old" personality, "new" personality, both good and bad.

But your partner is not "crazy," this is what is meant to happen. Midlife Crisis extracts a change, and disintegration is a part of it. Your partner is forced to look at every facet of their personality and make some permanent changes. The key to helping her/him through this is to accept what you see as it comes forth. Don't ridicule or shame her/him. You might see little kids picking their noses for example. Your partner might apologise for everything under the sun, and try really hard to make up for the damage, for a little while at least.

During **Stage TWO** of Acceptance, the temptation might come to want to go back to what s/he came out of. Your silence is most important during this time. All you can do is be understanding and patient with her/him as this must happen and s/he must come through this alone. Your partner will seem to be going backwards, but isn't. This is necessary to move forward.

It is during this time s/he will "revisit" all stages of the Midlife Crisis except Denial and shut the "doors" to each stage permanently one by one, never to return. If your partner gives in to temptation or get spooked by her/his final fears, s/he will run back into the tunnel a little way. But your partner can only run back as far as the doors have not been closed permanently. Most of the time s/he just runs back as far as Withdrawal, but will continue the process to come out once s/he feels "safe" to continue. So, your partner must be allowed to come through without interruption, no matter what happens.

Stage THREE involves the "Archway" mentioned in the stage of Withdrawal. All this time the "Midlifer" has been coming across this open field towards this archway where her/his "final fears" are located and finally begins to face these fears in full. Your partner may come out of the tunnel and face them before s/he shuts the door to Depression and Withdrawal or afterwards. But your partner will have to face them, nevertheless, before s/he exits to begin the complete healing process.

It will take time for the "Midlifer" to settle down. Even after your partner comes out of stage three of Acceptance, s/he might experience a final "rebelling" before settling down for good.

It is much like a teenager passing into adulthood. There are still final changes that must be made, especially for the one who has done so much damage during the crisis itself.

If your partner can settle everything within her~/himself, life should be marked with a sense of peace, instead of the anguish s/he has known for as long as the crisis has lasted. And your partner will have learned many things about life, and will be changed permanently, as s/he will never be the same as before, ever again.

MLC Timeline Guide Reminder

It may help to be reminded of the course of events and the time they can expect to take. This is not scientific, only put together from others' experiences, but nonetheless may help give you an idea of where you are right now.

Stage	Type	Period (Min/Max)	Total mths	Years
Stage 1	Denial	3—6 months	3 to 6	1
Stage 2	Anger	3—9 months	6 to 15	2
Stage 3	Replay	3—24 months	9 to 39	3
Stage 4	Depression	2—6 months	11 to 45	4
Stage 5	Withdrawal	3—12 months	14 to 57	5
Stage 6	Acceptance	3—12 months	17 to 69	6 to 7

You can now see that although we cannot be definite, a crisis could last anywhere from a year and a half to nearly seven years. There's that magic number seven again! The average given generally is five years, although in exceptional circumstances some may be shorter and others a lot longer. Also, remember that the first "bomb" usually falls around two years after the real start. If that is true and the "bomb" has just been dropped, prepare yourself for the rest of a long haul!

Stages Of MLC—The "Dummies Approach"

I know that the above was so serious and probably put you into shock, even though it may have made some sense and be able to identify with what you are going through. Here is an alternative view of MLC looked at from the perspective of a person going through a crisis. It is mildly amusing and contains a rough guide of how to behave to create the most damage. This section has been adapted from a personal posting on a forum website although it is now posted and copied in many other places.

How To Be A Proper MLC'er!

Chapter 1 Choosing The Correct Speech

There are four basic speeches for you to choose from to use on your spouse. They are:

a) I love you but don't know if I'm in love with you!

b) I've never loved you, and we should never have married!

c) We got married too young. I never knew anything else besides you!

d) You tricked me into marriage; I would never have done it otherwise!

Once you have decided on which speech to give, you need to cause as much anxiety in your spouse as you can before you actually deliver it. Continue to the next chapter for lessons in building anxiety.

Chapter 2 Lessons In Building Anxiety

You will find these lessons to be helpful in causing anxiety in your spouse and others (depending on the level of pain and damage you want to cause), not just prior to giving the speech, but throughout the course of your MLC.

Lesson 1 Monstrification Of Your Spouse

This is easy to accomplish. Simply think of only the "bad" things that your spouse has done throughout your entire relationship. Do you have one of those "angel" spouses? No problem, just remember how bad s/he always makes you feel. Do not, under any circumstance remember your spouse fondly, or anything s/he has done for you. Remember, s/he is going to be the cause of all of your problems and the target for your attacks, so it is imperative that you convince yourself of this first.

Lesson 2 Emotional Detachment

This will be very easy to do after accomplishing lesson 1. All you have to do is start reminding yourself that you don't care about her/him, what s/he feels, wants or if it hurts. Simple, isn't it! Every time you remind yourself of this, you will get further and further away from your relationship emotionally. Now, that wasn't too hard was it? On to lesson 3.

Lesson 3 Mass Confusion And Indecision

This lesson requires a little more thought and attention. You must constantly practise saying, "I don't know" to any and all questions. That is imperative!! Your spouse (and others) must never know precisely what is going on inside your head. Also, never let her/him know where you are going, where you have been, who you were with (this will go hand in hand with the lesson on the Other Person (OP), or whether or not s/he can expect you to return home at any time soon.

Lesson 4 Lies And Deceit

To get the most damage and cause the most pain, you must lie and deceive at every opportunity. And to really achieve hall of fame status, you should be very inept at it, so that everyone knows that you are lying, or suspects it, but can't prove it initially. This works very well for the following chapters, OP and Cake Eating.

Chapter 3 The Other Person (or OP)

Now it is time for you to succumb to temptation. You know that all those other women/men want you! They have been coming on to you for years!! It is time for you to give them their chance at having some of you. Make sure that you leave a very confusing trail for your spouse to follow. One that lets her/him suspect but have to dig and sneak (to make her/him feel worse about her~/himself) to find the information s/he needs to prove it. Hold out from admitting an affair as long as you can. Don't admit it ever, if you can get away with it!

Chapter 4 Cake Eating

This chapter is designed to string your spouse along in uncertainty as long as possible, because as long as there is hope, s/he won't be able to go out and find her/his own life and be fulfilled. Why should s/he get to do that, while you are so miserable? Your partner certainly shouldn't!! So, make sure that you are affectionate occasionally (not too often, as this will raise anxiety levels), that you drag your feet about making a decision on the marriage, and that you leave and come back several times (as many times as you can get away with!)

Chapter 5 History Revision

It is very important that you revise the life you have led with your spouse. You must use words like Always, Ever, Never and All of the Time. Always precede the statement with the terms: You, I, and We. As in "You always nag me," "I never ever (double bonus here) get to do what I want" and "We have to do what you want all of the time". This will help to make your spouse feel like the way you are behaving is all her/his fault and can cause her/him to feel even worse about her~/himself than s/he already did!

Chapter 6 It's All About You!

Remember this is all about you! What you want and need, right now! You shouldn't have to wait until you can afford something, just go out and get it! You deserve a new haircut, new clothes, and some new toys. You've worked for it. You would probably look great in that new convertible or on that new motorbike! So don't hesitate! You live in the here and now! Why wait until tomorrow?

Remember, the operative word is "crisis" and if you are in one, everyone else should have to ride the Roller coaster with you! It's no fun taking this ride alone, and you know what they say about misery loving company! Go on out there and get started, so much pain and damage, and so little time!

Chapter 7 Avoid, Ignore, and Run Away

This is to help you deal with the problems that your spouse will attempt to cause. We don't want you to have to "deal" with anything now, do we? You shouldn't have to "think" about any "issues" right now, except those that concern you "feeling good." The best way to handle this is to Avoid, Ignore, and Run Away. Any time someone tries to make you see a more "reasonable" stance on a subject, simply avoid making a reply … stare out into space, as if you are thinking about something important. Your partner will become uncomfortable and leave you alone.

If there are responsibilities that need your attention, simply ignore them. You don't have to do anything you don't feel like doing. And saving the best for last, run away! This can be accomplished in many different ways. OP's can help you run away from all of these "problems" as well as alcohol, drugs, new sports cars, motorbikes etc. The list is endless. Of course, you can always just leave, but remember not to let her/him know where you are going, and if or when you'll be back!

Chapter 8 Marriage Counselling and Therapists

Your spouse may ask you to go to counselling with her/him. This is only useful to make her or him feel better. It cannot possibly have anything to offer you so there is no reason for you to follow up with anything suggested. It doesn't matter to you. The only thing you should look for is more reasons or excuses for avoiding, running and ignoring (see previous chapter.)

Chapter 9 I Don't Have To If I Don't Want To And You Can't Make Me!

Remember that this is all about what you want and how you feel! No one else is important, so don't let her/him make you feel as if you have to listen to anything s/he says. Your spouse will try to help you of course, saying that s/he loves you. Don't believe her/him and don't let her/him get away with giving you unwanted advice. Let her/him know in the teenage vernacular that s/he can't make you do anything. This is important.

You must be as childish as possible! Any truly adult behaviour on your part will only convince her/him that you are listening to what is being said, and you will have to start back at the beginning. Of course, this technique can be used knowingly to cause more confusion and chaos, just beware of the danger. You don't actually want to start acting like an adult too soon!

Chapter 10 "How To Threaten" And/Or "How To Move Out".

Threaten to move out for weeks or months but don't. (*) Tell your spouse that you have too much on your plate right now to look for another place to live but will do so in 2 weeks time. After 2 weeks, repeat from (*).

If your partner wants to come too close to you, like having the cheek to enter a room to talk to you, tell her/him to stay away or you will move out. When your partner replies that you will move out anyway, tell her/him that you will move out faster if s/he comes any closer.

Chapter 11 Art Of Clinging

This is the art of clinging to the end of the mattress without falling off the matrimonial bed while still sharing it with your spouse.

Chapter 12 Advanced Lessons

This is usually reserved for those in more difficult situations, where the LBS'er has responded not by throwing you out, threatening to leave or filing for divorce, but instead persists in not only offering to co-operate but actually makes the changes you said you needed.

"I am tired of living like this/I don't want to live like this anymore/I am not going to live my life like this?" often could be coupled with another advanced tactic, "It's not you, it's me".

This line is most effective after the spouse has jumped through hoops and bent over backwards. It basically confirms that no matter what changes your spouse is willing to make, the incompatibility lies within you, who has no intention of or implied desire or ability to compromise.

Appendix

How To Make Your Spouse Think S/He Is Crazy

1. When confronted by the evidence of an emotional or physical affair, become very indignant. Stress that the your partner is obviously just a jealous person, and you are entitled to "buddies" of the opposite sex.

2. Never, ever answer the question, "Are you okay? Is there something wrong?" with a direct answer that might actually lead to a discussion that might help the marriage. Continue never to talk to your spouse, never give her/him a personal compliment or touch of affection and by all means work on the "cling to the edge of the mattress to avoid touching" manoeuvre that is proving to be so successful in making your spouse crazy.

3. Always bear in mind that your spouse will expect you to want to at least give them the chance to "fix" the marriage. Since you have already checked out emotionally (of course you must never tell her/him that!) you are under no obligation to actually listen to anything s/he says or acknowledge anything done.

This tactic is also extremely beneficial when your partner employs the MLC diet. When s/he loses a massive amount of weight and you are in earshot of someone who mentions the weight loss to your partner, just say casually "Are you losing weight? Why don't you ever tell me anything?"

4. Of course one of the most successful ways to drive her/him crazy may only be used when you have earned the MLC Black Belt. Go to marriage counselling for months, let her/him pour out her/his soul to you and the counsellor and let her/him believe s/he is actually accomplishing something. Then arrange things so the spouse finds you in your own home with another person. This will accomplish two things: a.) Your partner will finally have to understand how lucky you are to have found your "soul mate" and b.) Your partner will be doubly betrayed because she thought you were actually working on the marriage.

Don't Let Your Spouse Get Too Independent—Strategies For Sucking Your Partner Back In

1. Make negative comments about the OP or the chances that the relationship with the OP will succeed. However, under no circumstances make any commitment to end the relationship with the OP.

2. Make veiled hints about suicide or excessive drinking or drug use. Be erratic and hard to contact.

3. Do random acts of kindness such as working in the garden or something menial. That will keep your spouse confused and hopeful.

4. Make vague comments hinting that things might work out between you and your spouse in the future. However, under no circumstances take any actions to work anything out.

Custody

Using the kids to your advantage:

If you have children, they can be extremely useful for inducing fear and panic in your spouse. Recommended phrases include: "You're poisoning my kids against me", "You put that idea into their heads", and "You need to do [insert pertinent action here] for the sake of the kids." Remember that your spouse, being a responsible and loving person, is not only trying to cope with her/his own feelings, but also trying to protect the children and you can use that to your advantage.

Don't forget to use the fact that if you spend any time with your kids, you should get extra credit bonus "Good Parent" points from your spouse. It doesn't matter if you feed them ice cream for breakfast and have them watch "Night of the Living Dead" when they asked for "Cinderella." You just wanted to make them happy. Since you are the best judge of happiness that makes you the super parent. You can use this opportunity to talk your spouse down ("Isn't this more fun than what Mommy/Daddy would let you do?" "Mom/Dad doesn't know how to relax!") which of course, will be repeated back to your spouse in time so you get the benefit of destroying their self-esteem second hand.

Highly advanced MLC'ers may want to start casually using the word custody, but be very, very careful. While useful for sending your spouse into a state of panic, you certainly do not want to be responsible for a bunch of kids who will seriously cut into your personal fun time. The word custody should only be used in a casual tone of voice for the most devastating effect.

Button Pushing

You (the MLC'er) know a lot about your spouse. You know what pushes their buttons to get them both upset and/or happy. You have the power. You can do it! So using the kids to upset them is fair game (see section on how to use "custody" to upset them but do **not** take on the "custody"). And if that ever stops working, find something else. Suggestions might include pets, valuables in the home, personal appearance, family or career. Nothing is out of your reach since you have put in so many years getting to know your spouse. Use what you know!

The Blame Game

By now, you should be aware that all of this must be your spouse's fault. However, your spouse may not understand this completely yet, so you need to start planting the seeds.

There are several ingenious ways to put the blame on your spouse, and we will explore many of them.

Method 1: The Non-Blame Statement

"I'm trying not to blame you."

This statement implies that you are "not putting the blame on them" but on closer look (which your spouse is guaranteed to be doing) the words actually put all of the blame on the spouse (where of course we know it belongs!)

Method 2: The Passive Blame Statements

"I don't think that I can live with you."
"My opinion never mattered to you."
"I can't live like this."
"We are so different!"
"We rarely have fun anymore."
"I don't want to live this way anymore."
(There are many more I am sure you can think of.)

These are passive statements that don't actually assign blame to your spouse, but your spouse will definitely get the idea if you use them. Your partner can't help but see that it must be her/him that makes you feel this way.

Method 3: The Direct Blame Statement

"You never listen to me."
"You never put creases in my ironing."
"You only use pre-prepared salad."
"You never keep the house clean."
"You are going to do it your way anyway."

All of these are direct statements of blame. You should mix actual faults with things that don't really matter to make it much more confusing, and make your spouse feel as bad as possible about themselves.

Your spouse has probably already started doing the hard work to look inside her~/himself (which is an awful thought!) and will take on all of the faults you have listed to try and correct them. This will keep her/him occupied for a while, and you can avoid any serious relationship talk while s/he apologises for and try to fix all of her/his own faults. Make sure that you don't actually accept her/his apologies. That way you can continue to bring up whichever fault to slow down their self-improvement process. Remember, s/he is working on becoming a better human being and you wouldn't want that to happen too fast, as that would interfere with your ability to string her/him along.

Note: NEVER ACTUALLY ADMIT TO ANY FAULTS OF YOUR OWN!!!! REMEMBER, YOU DON'T HAVE ANY! YOU ARE THE GOOD ONE, AND HAD THE RIGHT TO HAVE AN AFFAIR, LIE, SPEND MONEY, OR ANY OTHER THING, BECAUSE S/HE IS THE ONE THAT IS BAD!!!

Let's not forget "We're just incompatible—we always were."

Also, when your partner starts to make changes, make sure you find fault with them, point out how it's "too little, too late" or wasn't what you meant at all. If all else fails, put the LBS'er down for being so willing to change her~/himself for your needs.

How to keep you spouse guessing; be very mean one minute threatening divorce etc. then next day be kind and sweet almost the way your spouse remembers you were … rinse and repeat …

How To Continue The Craziness Once Separation/Divorce Is Agreed Upon

1. Even though by now you, dear MLC'er, have done everything humanly possibly to convince your spouse that you do not love her/him and want out of the relationship, when the time comes to actually file, don't do it! This is the coup de gras of MLC. Absolutely do not take the initiative. This is a most vital and awesome crazy-maker. Holding out will force your by now totally devastated spouse to finally throw up her/his hands and seek legal counsel.

2. Once the LBS'er has had enough and decides that divorce is in her/his best interest, you have won huge points here. Refusing to be the one to file now puts you in the role of victim, bringing you all the attention and pity necessary to allow you to again regain your image of the abused one in all this. Now you can, with absolutely no guilt, tell everyone the divorce was your LBS'er's idea (which of course it was!) and they will assume that: a. the LBS'er lost all that weight and obviously has been involved in an affair, and b. the marriage ended because your

LBS spouse is going through a—Yes! **The pinnacle of craziness!**—A "Midlife Crisis."

The Shortest Guide To MLC Speak (Jocular!)

The shortest recommendation for an MLC'er is not to speak if at all possible. If you have to, try mumbling or use short sentences or single words if at all possible. "No," (never use positive words,) "Maybe" or "I don't know" should suffice. If that doesn't work, SHOUT or react, preferably in front of the kids or neighbours. You could also try speaking in another language that your partner does not know. This will show up yet another fault with her or him. Your partner does not share your interests, you are not compatible and s/he cannot be bothered to try and save the marriage. So there is no hope now, and this explains why you had to go to Thailand twice, of course just to see a friend!

I hope that you found that amusing, although unfortunately maybe too close to the truth. So there we go, all clear now and ready to go on?

So, Given All Of That, What Can or Should I Do?

There are strategies you (the LBS'er) can follow. These will be covered later. Healthy ones too! Hopefully you will learn all about them now. Remember the first rule is to detach with love. In equal first place, put **yourself** first from now on.

Three Elements Of True Love

True love has been defined elsewhere as consisting of three basic elements: heartfelt love, trust, and respect. These three cornerstones give completeness to a loving relationship. If any of these elements are missing, the relationship is in trouble. Perhaps this is why you can still feel love, while having lost trust or respect for your partner. And the same goes for your partner, saying that s/he still loves you, but is not "in love" anymore, despite her/his actions. Somewhere along the way respect and/or trust has disappeared between you.

Complementing v Completing

One of the hardest lessons to learn is that we should "complement" our partners in life, not look to "complete" each other. We all have strengths and weaknesses, and it is our ability to utilise each other's strengths that complements our being together. I think that many of us believe incorrectly that by having formed a unit, we think that we may assume the parts of our partners that we have found that were missing as "belonging" to us. This is a huge mistake.

In reality, we should look to each other for continuing and loyal support, appreciating the different aspects that we can bring to the relationship, without assuming "control" or "ownership" of the other, or thinking that because we have seen how it has been done once or twice, we know exactly what to do in the future, thereby possibly negating the need for the other.

Appreciating The Differences

We are all different, as hinted to above. Instead of taking the statement "We are so different!" at face value, it comes down to personal attitude and expectations. Understanding that we are different but wanting to learn from and share each other's values, experiences and abilities can and will make our partnerships stronger. Wouldn't it be boring if we were all the same with nothing left to learn from others?

However, there are those who will try to pick up new skills all the time, moving on when s/he believe that all has been gained from involvement in the "experience." Boredom and dissatisfaction may have set in, and new "challenges" may await, which s/he believe can only be gained from relationships with new people.

I just like to believe that you don't have to leave your marriage to find this out. That having made such a huge life-long commitment to each other, you should be able to try to learn new things together or singly, with your common interests and objectives always remaining at heart.

I guess it comes down to truly appreciating those differences, not rejecting or at worst becoming jealous of them or each other in the process.

Why Won't S/He Speak To Me?

Quite simply, your partner has nothing to say to you at the moment. Your partner also doesn't know what to say to you. At present your partner is not in love with you, does not think that s/he loves you anymore and doesn't even consider you to be a friend, let alone her/his best friend. This is in spite of saying initially "I want to stay friends." Your partner is looking at it now from the other side of the coin.

If you were to ask her/him how s/he would react to being rejected in this way, to being unloved, cheated on etc. that is exactly how your partner believes s/he would react. You may even have agreed this basic principle together in the past. Your partner cannot see why you would want anything to do with her/him anymore. Your partner simply does not understand or respect you for acting any differently.

Why Doesn't S/He Want To See Me?

The best way to describe this is to think how a small child who has been naughty covers its eyes, thinking that because s/he can't see you, you can't see her/him, even if in clear view. Your partner cannot face up to what s/he has done or is doing. In seeing you your partner will see her~/himself, have to face up to facts, possible failure and betrayal. Your partner thinks that by not seeing you s/he will not have to face up to the past and the present. Once you are in front of her/him, s/he has to come up with something. And because s/he doesn't want to, will do anything to stop having to! If your partner has to, s/he will go on the attack. After all, attack is known as the best form of defence! Your partner believes that by having nothing to do with you unless s/he has to, the problem might go away of its own accord.

Also, despite your strong feelings, your partner might not consider you to be a friend anymore. Your partner says that s/he does not feel a need to see you, to speak to you, to share thoughts or any time with you. In fact, s/he might even deliberately avoid you. This may be her/his coping strategy, to avoid and run away. Your partner cannot cope with seeing you!

It is extremely hard to cope with utter rejection, but remember this is not your fault. As hard as it is to handle and understand, **you** are not a bad person!

There could be another aspect to this too, and one that may be hard to comprehend. As long as the MLC'er keeps her/his "two lives" separate, it could be that subconsciously in the far back of her/his mind that "options" are still being kept open, if only slightly, and never admitted or revealed to you. That after a while, should the new life not work out to her/his satisfaction, then as you will not have been "exposed" to or involved in any part thereof, there may be just a chance in the future of rekindling yours. For example, has your partner ever told you "Although I know what I feel now, I don't know what I will be doing or where I will be in three, five or ten years time?"

Noticing The Changes

Now, you know that you might have seen significant changes in your partner. What happens when s/he sees changes in you? Especially if you have worked hard on yourself and made some or all of the "changes" that your partner said s/he found wanting in your relationship. Firstly, s/he might feel very uncomfortable. S/he might already be involved with someone else and just seeing the "new you" might be very disconcerting. For this reason, s/he might have to come up with another list of faults that are "wrong" with you, just to send you on your way and justify her/his continued behaviour. This also might give added impetus to the perceived need to "stay away from you." "Out of sight, out of mind!" also springs to the fore. You cannot win in this situation. Don't think you can.

The lesson to learn here is make changes by all means if **you** think they are necessary, but only for **you** and not anyone else. You may have learned some important lessons from the relationship that will make you a better partner for whoever you might be with in the future, whether it be your ex or someone new.

Why Does S/He Still Want To Be "Friends?"

LBS—Initially at least, your partner knows that even though s/he is choosing to blame you for everything that is wrong with your relationship, you have really done nothing fundamentally incorrect. Your partner knows that s/he is in the wrong. Your partner really does care for you and doesn't want you to suffer. Because s/he has managed to get over you so easily, it should be the same for you. Little does s/he know!

Your partner believes that by offering friendship in the first place, s/he will stay in your "good books" and assist you to get on with your own life. This changes with time. If you continue to hang on, to cling to, to try and fix things, s/he gets bored. It is interfering with her/his ability to get on with the new life. After what you consider to be a short time, s/he reduces the offer of close friendship to just friends, and even that may and probably will be taken back. Your partner loses patience with you, thinking that you are too weak, not showing certain strength of character.

After all, would your partner want to maintain any form of friendship with someone behaving the way that s/he has? You know the answer. In truth, your partner has proved her~/himself unworthy of that high honour.

You must decide whether **you** want to be friends or not now. It is up to **you!**

MLC—You may no longer consider your partner to be part of your life, and for this reason you may have decided not to be friends with her/him, regardless of how s/he feels about you.

Why Does S/He Say That S/he Wants Me To Get On With My Own Life?

LBS—Even though we might have that impression, your MLC'er does not hate you. Not in the normal course of events. Your partner does hate her~/himself for what has been or is being done (even if s/he does not acknowledge this at the start.) Your partner initially believes that you too still deserve the best that life has to offer and to be as happy as s/he is or at least pretends to be. This is why s/he encourages you to take steps to your own freedom. It also relieves your partner of any responsibility or reduces her/his feelings of guilt, or so s/he thinks.

Of course when you do get on with your life your partner's mindset may change. It might come as a shock to her/him, but s/he now sees your independence, the fact that you can manage without her/him. This was not part of "the overall plan." This might lead to various results. Either your partner can become jealous, realising that someone else wants you as much as s/he used to. Your partner might try to make amends or just become angry. Now your partner can start blaming you all over again for newly found reasons, fully justifying what has been done. Your partner might use your new life as justification not only of her/his own previous and current behaviours, but also in divorce proceedings that s/he might choose to initiate against **you** for adultery!

MLC—You might be getting on with your life quite happily, and would like to see your former partner being happy too, but not with you!

Why Does S/He Say S/he Can't Be Her~/himself When S/he Is With Me?

An LBS'er may say that their partner has said or implied that s/he can't be her~/himself when with her/him, that her/his true self is being suppressed. The truth is that s/he feels very uncomfortable. Your partner believes that her/his new "persona" is so different and that s/he would have to act in a certain way, one that is now alien to her or him. Your partner fears being "dragged" down or pulled back by you and your presence to their former self. S/he can not believe that you will find her/him acceptable anymore. Your partner might not think that s/he comes up to your "standards." This is all in her/his head, not yours. Your partner might also think that s/he has changed and "advanced" so much, while you haven't, you still seem "stuck", and they have left you way behind. You might be seen as "safe and secure", not exciting! You never know, **you** might like what you see, **you** might not. It should be up to **you** to decide, not her or him!

I Want You To Take The Blame!

There is also a "counter-strategy" argument to the answers to the last two questions. So far, we have seen that this "Transition" is not your fault. If there is any fallout, the MLC'er is responsible. Your partner has now shown that s/he does not have the courage to face you or her~/himself or to be honest for her/his actions, both verbal and physical. Your partner may want you to take the lead, to say that you have had enough, for you to walk away and initiate divorce proceedings. This way s/he can fully justify to her~/himself and others that you are to blame, that you do not want to work on the relationship, even to try or be together anymore and that **you** filed for divorce!

The 10 Commandments Of Breaking Up

These rules do not apply specifically to MLC, but because they apply to the break up of relationships and are so relevant they are worthy of sharing with you. This was forwarded to me anonymously:

1. **Thou shalt not call him/her.** Yes, there is a reason why you broke up and a lot of people make the mistake of breaking up and then entering into a "friends" dialogue. People are very keen to maintain some level of contact and pull out the friend card in particular as it makes them feel like they aren't as awful as they think you might believe they are. This also keeps a foothold in your life that often ends up stopping you from moving on. Whatever reason (or excuse) you believe is a good idea to call, whether you think s/he will change his mind if s/he hears from you or that you'll feel good, is not a reason to call. The initial surge of hope or elation you feel will be replaced by a slump, which will take you to a lower place mentally than you were before you made the call. If you need to get something from her or him, get someone else to sort it out for you.

2. **Thou shalt remain mature.** Cutting up her/his possessions may help you take out your revenge but you'll probably find yourself in court. Don't be petty, don't let your friends be petty on your behalf with your interests at heart and don't act like a gangster. Revenge may feel like a dish best served cold but it's better to leave it off the menu all together. Maintaining dignity and her/him know that you have moved on will actually reward you better in the long run. Let her/him regret the loss of someone so great rather than have her/him thank her/his lucky stars that s/he got rid of you.

3. **Thou shalt not have some post break-up sex.** If sex was the only thing holding you together in the first place, that was not a good thing. If it was that great and so important you wouldn't have broken up. If you think that giving her/him a bit more pleasure will have her/him crawling back to you, it won't. Sex is a temporary, albeit pleasurable remedy but you can't shag her/him back into your relationship. It has been said: "Why buy the cow when you can drink the milk for free?"

4. **Thou shalt not email or text.** This may seem like a less scary option than calling but it's just something else to make you feel like bad as you agonise over the tone of the reply (that's if s/he replies at all), the length of the reply or even how long it takes to get a response. Again, if you need to get something, like your possessions, have a trusted friend collect them for you.

5. **Thou shalt not accidentally on purpose keep on going to the places that you know s/he goes to.** Trust me, the initial high you get when you see her/him is likely to be replaced by paranoia, insecurity and misery as you wonder what s/he is thinking or even worse, what s/he is saying about you to friends, or worrying about who that person is that s/he is speaking to. Even if you went there first, it's better just to steer clear. However, if you want to go anywhere or see anyone, it is up to you. Your partner must and will not dictate your life.

6. **Thou shalt not cling to pathetic signs that you're getting back together.** The horoscopes, the psychic, the hopefulness of friends and family who actually don't know anything, magpies, and anything else that makes you think you're on your way back to love will only lead to disappointment. Deal only with the facts.

7. **Thou shalt not hide away.** Trust me when I say that it is very likely that when you're lying around in your PJs, sobbing your heart out, stuffing your face

or not eating at all, sitting by the phone … s/he is not! I'm not suggesting that every last woman or man is cold, but when s/he dumps you, s/he doesn't tend to react like many of us would to a break up. The words "short attention span" spring to mind, which means that even if it hurts, s/he is unlikely to be locking her~/himself away; in fact s/he will be living her/his life to the full.

8. **Thou shalt accept the break up as final.** Don't break up and spend your mental energies clinging to the hope that you will be getting back together. You are not a yo-yo or a boomerang to be picked up and discarded at will. Instead of clinging to hope and living your life with a view to her/him making her/his way back into it, take the decision as final. Of course there is a slim chance that s/he will come back one day with a firm decision and a resolve to want to get together. If the issues that broke you up in the first place are resolved, possibly with the help of a therapist, you may choose to try and reconcile. Just don't wait for this to happen and build your own life. And of course, by the time s/he might come back, you may not even want her/him anymore.

9. **Thou shalt not return her/his calls.** People are mostly made up of water and the rest is ego. Your partner needs to think that you want her/him, that you are pining for her/him and that your whole life revolves around waiting for her/him to dignify you with contact. Your partner wants to move on but check that you're not and s/he likes to make sure that you haven't moved on to the next guy or girl. Your partner might rear her/his ugly head when s/he knows you have started to want someone else. I'm sure that your partner is concerned to an extent about how you are but a lot of it is about reassuring her~/himself that s/he is not a "nasty" person. A lot of people like to think only the best of her~/himself. Don't reply to inane e-mails either. If you worry about feeling like a cruel person, give yourself licence to avoid contact by telling your partner that for the sake of you both (it's all in the wording) that it would be better if you didn't have contact for a while. People don't go from being lovers to friends in a blink of an eye and these things take time so s/he will just have to put up with the life choice s/he made. Of course you might need to respond to calls regarding kids or "business" related issues, and these should not be ignored or avoided.

10. **Thou shalt recognise when s/he is behaving badly.** One of the perturbing things about break ups is that even in the face of you being treated like dirt at the time of the break up or after, you might not take the hint very easily. You may blame yourself. You might lose self-esteem and throw in all self-respect too.

Recognise that your partner is behaving in an unacceptable manner, lose your respect for her/him as soon as you can and keep your self-esteem intact. Believe it or not, when a person behaves like this, s/he is doing you a massive favour by showing you her/his real side. Trust me, if you take her/him back while or after treating you badly without significant change in behaviour or attitude taking place, you have to accept responsibility for writing the script of your future. And no prizes for guessing how that is going to work out!

Now, as an aside, I know that there are some of you that will not be able to resist making contact. I was one of them, guilty as charged! However it is strongly recommended that there must be a minimum period of absolutely no contact. This will give both parties time to think and act alone, to find out exactly what it is like not having each other to call, ask advice or get opinions from.

How Long Does The "Crisis" Last?

As mentioned before, but well worth repeating, every crisis is different, although they all seem to have remarkable similarities. From the experience of many others, an average of five years seems to be the norm. Do remember, this is not from the date of the initial "bomb" being dropped, but rather from when the crisis commenced, which could be up to two years before the explosion itself.

Can MLC Be Prevented?

Want a short answer? No, not really! Neither should one attempt to. It can be delayed or prolonged though. It is a natural (though in the case of MLC seemingly unnatural) human growth pattern. We all go through periods of change. It is how we deal with it that differs from person to person, turning a transition into what becomes a crisis.

Coping Strategies—What Not To Do

It is important to know what does and doesn't work, so you don't waste your time and energy "punching the wind." This has been adapted from a posting on the midlife crisis forum.

We will start with a list of the **DO NOTS**:

DO NOT cry in front of your W/H. This will make you look needy. MLC'ers do not like needy. S/he will not appreciate it or the feelings behind it.

DO NOT beg your W/H to stay. If s/he talks about moving out, let her/him go. If you beg, once again you look needy.

DO NOT say "I love you" to your W/H. It is hard not to, but you have to for two reasons: firstly, these words put pressure on your partner and will make her/him run away from you even faster and secondly, you won't do yourself any favours. There is no worse reply to an honest and heartfelt "I love you" than a simple "I know" or no response whatsoever.

DO NOT yell, blame or fight with your W/H. Go to your private diary or an MLC website to get it all out on your thread. If you fight with your W/H you will only push her/him further away and possibly give her/him another justification for leaving you, which gets me to the next point.

DO NOT defend yourself. While In MLC the W/H will blame you for everything. Your partner will try and fight with you to justify what s/he is doing. Do not take the bait. If s/he blames you for anything, all you can say is "I am sorry you feel that way," and then walk away. If you defend yourself it gets her/him even angrier.

DO NOT snoop. Your partner might have an affair. Remember if s/he does that the other man or woman is only a plaster or Band-Aid to the problems. So when I say do not snoop that means; do not look at mobile phones, check the pockets, smell the shirts, look for lipstick marks, check the briefcase or follow her/him in your car. In the long run you will be the one that will be hurt more.

DO NOT judge or point fingers. This means don't tell your partner what s/he is doing is wrong. Trust me, your partner knows but cannot help how s/he feels. You will only make her/him more angry and rebellious.

DO NOT tell everyone you know about your W/H. Most MLC'ers do not like being talked about. Again you will only push her/him further away.

DO NOT try and be a hero. Do not go to your W/H's best friend and try and talk to them. That is a big no no! The MLC'er will find out and feel you are invading her/his space.

DO NOT show anger at your W/H. You will learn how to do this in time. Express it elsewhere. Buy a punch bag, a pillow, any thing or place you can let out that emotion, safely.

DO NOT buy gifts or cards, anything that would have to do with being a couple, this is pressure to an MLC'er. No Valentine, Birthday, Anniversary or Xmas cards, nothing that gives your game away.

DO NOT think this is your fault, it is not. The sooner you realise this, the sooner you will heal.

DO NOT tell your W/H that he or she is in MLC. At worst s/he will deny it. Your partner will think (or think s/he knows) that you are wrong. S/he might be angry that you think this. Your partner might think that s/he has experienced change but it is all over now, little realising that s/he is only part way through.

DO NOT tell her/him about forums, discussion groups etc. This is for your own good. This can be a counter strategy. Your partner may learn new behaviours that justify her/his actions. If s/he really wants to find out more, excellent. Let her/him find them on her/his own only when ready to.

DO NOT give your partner books on MLC. Do not give her/him any information on MLC. This may give her/him a feeling of justification and permission to carry on, because it is only a natural process isn't it/It happens to everyone/You can't stop it? etc. On the other hand, your partner may read **one** thing that s/he does not agree with, and therefore assume s/he is not going through **any** of this process at all!

DO NOT try to get her/him to go to a doctor or for counselling. MLC'ers do not like being told what to do.

DO NOT question her/him. This means do not ask your partner where s/he is, what time s/he will be home, who s/he is talking to on the phone, why s/he is wearing that shirt or dress, why s/he is so angry, and so on. Just leave her/him alone.

Before moving on just remember this. People do not willingly associate with unhappy, depressed or negative people. We all prefer to be surrounded by happy individuals. We all prefer positive company. We do not want to be with people who are always looking down or back. We like to be with bright, alert, forthright people. We do not like to be seen with others who look a mess. We like to be seen with people who are attractive, clean and well dressed. Like attracts like. This applies to your partner too. Get the hints?

Coping Strategies—What To Do

Now that we might have completely destroyed your preliminary plan of action, you may well be asking, "Well, what can or should I do then?"

DO make sure you take care of yourself during this time.

DO make sure you
- Eat
- Sleep
- Rest as often as possible if you cannot sleep

DO read as much as you can on MLC.

DO make sure you keep your mind and body active during this time. Join a gym, a walking group, take up a new hobby, do some project around the house that maybe you have put off, go back to study a favourite or new subject, and get out with friends or family.

DO make sure you give your W/H lots and lots of space.

DO make sure if you have children, to look out for them. While in crisis a lot of MLC'ers are not the best parents. S/he can only think for the moment and can only worry about her~/himself. You will need to be the rock for your children. Look out for them. Worry only about you and your children.

DO have a good friend, family member or counsellor you can talk to. You will need a shoulder or an ear from someone.

DO get to a doctor anytime you start to feel down, depressed or low. There are good Anti-Depression medications out there and you can get something to help cope.

DO protect yourself when it comes to money. While in MLC many partners like to spend like there is no tomorrow. Please keep an eye on your credit cards and bank accounts. If you can, open your own.

DO make sure you are good to yourself during this time. Treat yourself to something nice now and then. You have to look out for yourself. Your W/H will not be able or want to do it at this time.

DO all your venting on an MLC board, not at your W/H. This is important. Let others with experience of MLC help you.

How To Deal With Feelings Of Wanting Revenge!

It is only natural for you to want your partner to feel at least some of the pain and anguish that you do. However, there is no need for you to take revenge personally, and I encourage you **not** to take any unnecessary action.

Whether you believe in God or a Higher Power, let me assure you that either is doing this on your behalf. You do not have to participate. You may not believe it now, but there are forces at work! Look closely, it might come in the strangest ways. Your partner might have to move home, change jobs, experience illness and even have problems with transport. Feel free to name it! Your partner will have to assume many elements of management of their lives and business that you previously took care of.

Your partner has to learn a lot of new things and might make mistakes that you will not be around to solve or prevent. Her/his new relationship/s might seem to start off fantastically well, but after a while they too could become stale or have problems. Your partner will need to meet and associate with the family of their new "significant others." Both sets of children might resent the involvement of someone new, plus s/he might need to deal with the other partner's ex (or exes!) from time to time and the associated problems they bring up. Your partner might have to extricate her~/himself from some or many commitments that s/he makes during this time. Some will have been made on the spur of the moment, some planned. Your partner will have to think about replacing your income to meet her/his needs. S/he will have problems relating to her/his own children, family and friends. Your partner will assume a lot of responsibility and undergo considerable stress. S/he stands to lose a lot of her/his long-established relationships and support network. Your partner has chosen to ignore and reject her/his previous life. This has tremendous impact on and consequences for the future.

You might experience short-term satisfaction from what happens and when it does, but later become very upset yourself. After all, you probably don't wish your ex-partner any real harm!

Stages Of Grief

It is also vital to understand the process that we go through when we experience grief of any sort, be it death or loss of a loved one in any way:

- **Denial**—You can't believe this is true, so you keep on going back to check and try again (I can't believe this is happening!),

- **Anger**—First of all with yourself, then against others or the circumstances (Why is this happening to me?),

- **Bargaining**—Trying to work it out (I promise I can and will change if only I have another chance),

- **Depression**—Sadness at the loss, trying to work out what you can possibly do (I don't care about anything in the world anymore),

- **Acceptance**—Coming to the realism of the true situation (I am getting over this and am ready to make my way ahead now.)

This "definition", although printed in many places, was brought to us by Dr. Elizabeth Kübler-Ross and is fully explained in her book.

It is thought that dealing with grief only really begins after these five stages have been completed, in other words when you have reached the acceptance phase. This has been described with the acronym **TEAR**:

- **T** = To accept the reality of the loss,

- **E** = Experience the pain of the loss,

- **A** = Adjust to the new environment without the lost object or person,

- **R** = Reinvest in the new reality.

And yes, there may be many tears, and they are a very healthy form of expression, for women and men. It is also virtually impossible to give a firm time-frame for the above. They might not happen in sequence, some may occur together, and there is no confirmed time frame for any of them. It will all depend on the severity and importance of the loss that is the cause of your grief.

Another categorisation of the grief process comes from Dr. Robert Temes:

- **Numbness**—where you just "function" and separate yourself from society,
- **Disorganisation**—where you experience intense feelings of loss and
- **Reorganisation**—where you attempt to re-enter "normal" life.

I don't think we can ever hope to forget the person or situation that we grieve for. If lucky, we remember the good times more often than the bad, and it does mean we will have times when waves of grief come back to haunt us.

Divorce

Many believe that divorce is an easy option. Let me assure you that in addition to possible high financial costs, however simple you or s/he may be led to think it will be, a lot of what has been hidden will come out, before, during and afterwards. Old wounds will surface and need to be addressed. Supporting information will be revealed. It can become very messy. Once lawyers get involved, the gloves are off and both lawyers will fight to get the best deal possible, at the expense of either spouse. They are independent and seemingly unfeeling. This is what they are paid to do. The consequences of divorce are enormous, and will affect you, your spouse and family members. It will not all be over when you receive the formal papers. It is very likely that you will still have contact, especially if children are involved. There is no such thing as a truly amicable divorce. At least one of the partners will be very hurt by this process. Probably both of you!

People cannot run away or hide from themselves, their issues or problems by getting a divorce, as much as they try to or wherever they go. Divorce may not bring the immediate "happiness" expected. Unless addressed properly, the same or similar problems tend to come back time and time again. Only time will tell and this is a very harsh lesson.

"Right, take one pace for each year we spent together and two for each child, I really **don't** want to hurt you!"

CHAPTER 5

▼

DETACHING WITH LOVE (PROBABLY THE JOINTLY MOST IMPORTANT STEP!)

Detachment is a most important strategy for your recovery from this situation. It is so important that it is well worth devoting a chapter to on its own.

You will see that detachment is vital in your path forward and must be taken very seriously. It is a vital strategy for your health and sanity. Without detaching emotionally you will not begin to deal with the horrors of MLC. At the same time there is no doubt that it is very hard to do.

I must add the very important point that detaching from someone is not the same as abandoning her or him. You may choose to never abandon your partner totally or even think that you are doing so. Abandoning means never having anything to do with your partner. So, think of it this way if you want to try to save your relationship; detach with love, not without it. Maintain your underlying love for your partner, as long as you are willing and able to. The information has been adapted from the various websites mentioned in the credits, all of who give much the same useful guidelines.

What Is Detaching?

Detaching in its simplest form is letting go, distancing and separating yourself from the close attachment you feel to your partner or the problem/s you are trying to resolve. Imagine that you are currently inside a triangle or bubble with your partner, surrounded by all the issues you face and having a choice of either fighting to keep yourself alive inside, or thinking about getting away from it all. Now, take it a step outside and look back in. What you see inside now is just a little bit of you and your entire partner surrounded by all that murk. You may now be able to be more rational, not allowing all those feelings to affect you directly. You can select and analyse each and every aspect or decision that you choose to see clearly, separately, rationally and effectively.

Perhaps, before doing this and to get you in the correct mindset, think about someone else's situation. You are now most definitely outside of their triangle. Do you think that you may be able to give advice that you think is very clear, decisive and straightforward? How you would deal with their situation if requested to give advice? Perhaps you have already been asked to do this.

Detaching allows you to do exactly this. By consciously putting yourself on the outside, you automatically give yourself the power and control you need, without being affected by the turmoil and confusion that reigns inside the triangle itself.

What Is It All About?

Let's define what detaching allows you to do, in relatively short statements:

- By detaching you will allow individuals to be themselves.

- You will be able to hold back from feeling the need to rescue, save or "fix" your partner. You will give her/him "space" to be her~/himself.

- You will disengage from a totally integrated or dependent relationship with your partner.

- You will accept that you cannot control your partner or her/his actions.

- You will manage to develop and maintain a safe emotional distance from your partner that you have previously given a lot of power to.

- You will be able to establish firm emotional boundaries between you and your partner, and develop your own sense of independence.

- You will be free to feel your own feelings and not feel guilty or responsible for the failures of your partner.

- You will be able to hold onto your bond of love without rescuing or controlling your partner.

- You will view all things in a healthy, rational way.

- You will develop the ability to protect your emotions and prevent greater devastation.

- You will let the person you love and care for accept personal responsibility.

- You will allow your partner to become who s/he "really is" rather than what you "want her/him to be."

- You will avoid being hurt, abused, neglected or taken advantage of.

Although you will still have feelings for your partner, they will be controlled and you will have given both the "freedom" to become individuals, to succeed or fail apart from each other.

You will have allowed both of you to assume personal responsibility to become unique, independent and autonomous beings, with no fear of retribution or rebuke from each other.

What Are The Risks, If You Do Not Detach?

There are significant risks associated with not detaching:

- Your partner may become over-dependent on you, or you on her/him.

- You may run the risk of being manipulated to do things for the other that you really have no wish to. You may perform tasks as a result of intimidation.

- You may feel powerless and under your partner's control.

- You may obsess about "fixing" her/him.

- You may be blind to the reality that there are things you need to let go of to become healthy and coping.

- You may be too easily influenced by a perception of helplessness that is being projected onto you.

- You might be caught up in the ideal of making everything perfect for your partner.

- You run the risk of becoming out of control and losing self-esteem and self-respect. You might put off decisions or following through, thinking of the consequences.

- You might feel so guilty and emotionally dependent that the state of your relationship may worsen.

- Finally, you run a big risk of losing your autonomy and independence, deriving your sense of value only from an unhealthy relationship.

Why Is Detachment A Control Issue?

The following will demonstrate why elements of detachment are directly linked to control issues:

- Detachment removes external events that might control your life.

- It strengthens your ability to take control.

- By remaining attached, you remain firmly under your partner's control.

- Keeping your "distance" emotionally or physically does require self-discipline. Inability to do this indicates that you might be "out of control."

- If you do not detach, you might remain powerless over this behaviour.

- You might feel brainwashed or in a trance when you are with your partner.

- You might feel intimidated to stay deeply attached for fear of harm to either of you. You may allow yourself to be manipulated.

- You may be so busy dealing with her/him that you divert attention from yourself.

These are the major issues that show you how not detaching affects your ability to be in control of **your** future.

What Thinking Leads To An Inability To Detach?

The following is a list of questions and statements that you may ask yourself that stop you detaching from your partner. However as you will see, there is an answer for each that clearly indicates that your fears might have been irrational.

Q	What will s/he do without me, if I stop being involved?
A	*Does it matter? Your partner has said that s/he **doesn't** want your involvement.*
Q	My partner needs me and that must be enough to justify my involvement?
A	*No it isn't! Nobody **needs** someone else, you might wish it to be so.*
Q	What if s/he commits suicide because of my detachment?
A	*It is very unlikely, and if s/he attempts to, you could not have stopped her/him anyway!*
Q	I would feel so guilty if anything happened to him/her.
A	*Everyone is responsible for her~/himself from now on.*
Q	My partner has been so dependent on me, what will s/he do now?
A	*Your partner survived before you, and will continue to. And so will you!*
Q	I need him/her as much as s/he needs me.
A	*Not true, no one **needs** someone else.*
Q	I can't control myself because every day I promise, "today is the day."
A	*You need to make a decision and follow it through, as difficult as it may be.*
Q	Being detached seems so cold and aloof. Isn't it one-way or the other?
A	*No, don't confuse detachment with abandonment.*
Q	If I leave the relationship too soon, I may not have given my partner enough chance.
A	*When is too soon? Only do this when you have had enough.*

Q	How can detachment help? My partner needs more help, not less.
A	*By finding her~/himself this will help her/him find what s/he wants out of life.*
Q	Detachment sounds so final. It sounds so distant. It seems so unnatural.
A	*It is not. It is a step in either recovering your relationship or yourselves.*
Q	You never want someone in a relationship with you to be detached emotionally, so how can it be a good thing?
A	*Your partner does not currently want to be in a relationship with you and has said so. Let her/him find out what life is like in reality.*
Q	The family that plays together stays together. All for one and one for all.
A	*When you are together yes! When not, no!*
Q	If one hurts, we all do. How can you have a good relationship unless you share everything, good and bad?
A	*You are not in a good relationship at the moment. You must allow your partner to be her~/himself.*
Q	When s/he is in trouble, how can I ignore pleas for help?
A	*Your partner has got her~/himself into trouble, and must sort it out.*
	Now you've had a chance to think about them, weren't they irrational thoughts?

How Do I Develop Detachment?

There are several things you will need to do and practise in order to develop true detachment:

- Establish a set of emotional boundaries between you and your partner with whom you have become overly entangled or dependent on.

- Take back all power over your feelings from your partner who in the past you have given the control to affect your emotional wellbeing.

- Hand over to your Higher Power your partner who you would like to see changed but whom you cannot change yourself.

- Commit to your own recovery and self-health by admitting to yourself and your Higher Power that there is only one person you can change and that is you. That you need to let go of the "need" to fix, change, rescue, or heal your partner.

- Recognize that it is "unhealthy" to believe that you have the power of control, enough to fix, correct, change, heal, or rescue your partner if s/he does not see a need to change her~/himself.

- Recognize that you need to be healthy yourself in order for another to recognise that there is something that needs changing by and for her~/himself.

- Continue to own your feelings as your responsibility and do not blame your partner for the way you feel.

- Accept personal responsibility for your own unhealthy actions, feelings, and thinking. Stop looking at your partner to blame for your condition.

- Accept that addictive fixing, rescuing, enabling are not healthy behaviours and strive to extinguish them in your relationship to your partner.

- Accept that your partner in your past and current life is irrational, unhealthy and has brought toxic influences into your life. Label her/him honestly for what s/he is, and stop minimizing her/his negative impact on your life.

- Reduce the impact of guilt and other irrational beliefs. These may impede your ability to develop detachment in your life.

- Practise "letting go" of the need to correct, fix, or make better your partner in life over which you have no control or power to change.

Detaching The Person From The Event/s

So far, we have been trying to separate the person her~/himself from the event/s. This has attempted to enable you to continue to feel love for your partner despite her/his actions. This would be ideal. It also provides you with the best chance for possible reconciliation at a later date, not that this can be guaranteed.

Of course a time may come when you wish to detach completely. For example, when you have reached your limit and had enough. Too much has happened and you make a conscious decision to go your own way. You can't and don't feel any love for your partner anymore. Perhaps more importantly, you don't wish to. Your partner may no longer be worthy of your love and devotion, in your eyes at least. Remember that you do not **need** someone; you merely **desire** her or him. You can survive without her/him. You certainly did beforehand. You have now moved from detachment to abandonment, complete detachment equals abandonment.

When the time comes that you wish to fully detach from your partner, at least you will know that you have given any chance of resolving the situation your best shot.

Detaching v Abandoning And Letting Go

It is worth reinforcing and distinguishing between detachment and abandonment. Think of a kite for example. In this explanation imagine the kite as your partner, and the string as responsibilities and control issues. The more string you have the more control issues and responsibilities you carry. The more you release, the more you give back to your partner. You are attached to the kite by this piece of string with control issues and responsibility. The wind is the MLC. When a strong wind blows, you "let go" of more string. This means you place fewer demands on the kite. You still remain "attached" but are now further away and detaching from close contact. This demonstrates detachment.

If you pull too hard against the wind to try and bring it back to you, the string might snap and you will probably lose the kite. When you let go of the string completely, the kite disappears off into the distance and you have no more contact with it. You may never find it again. You have then let go completely. You have abandoned the kite. This simile could apply to your relationship!

Remember this is all about protecting you. If you try to hold on against the strong wind it might unbalance you or pull you over. You want to stay upright and in control of yourself!

Finally, if the wind gusts too strongly you may run out of string completely. In other words too much has happened or is happening and you have nothing left to give. Having released all that you have, you have no option but to let go completely. Abandon it! Remember to save yourself!

How To Cope With Being Abandoned

You may well feel that you have been abandoned now. When and if you are, there is a helpful description of five stages that have to be passed through. They happen repeatedly in cycles although they should get more infrequent and less intense as time goes on. This explains why you might think you are fine one day then down in the dumps or back at the beginning the next. Under those circumstances, you have probably entered a new cycle.

The first is **Destructing**. This is when you first process and try to analyse the terrible thoughts about your situation. You may feel total shock, a lot of pain, panic about the past and the future, experience despair and feel totally helpless.

Then you go into **Retreating**. When you retreat and withdraw you may feel a craving for your partner, your need for attachment and bonding. These feelings are stronger than ever they were, and are quite natural.

Afterwards you begin **Internalising**. This is the stage when you blame yourself for everything that has gone wrong, what you could or should have done, expressing your anger at yourself for your failings, and lose self-esteem and self-confidence in the process.

You feel **Anger**. After you have faced your demons, the anger that you have been aiming at yourself turns in direction. You know that much of this was not your fault and you don't want to accept the blame totally or anymore. You become very angry with your partner, starting to vent and externalise your feelings. This is very healthy and you stop beating yourself up for things you are not responsible for. You may not wish to face your partner directly with the anger you feel. Instead of verbalising your thoughts, top tips include writing them down in your personal diary or a letter and burning it or beating a pillow with your fists to let it all out physically.

Lastly you experience **Constructing.** Because you have begun to vent your rage and anger, you no longer carry it internally. You have begun to let go. The additional free space it gives to your head allows you to rise out of this intense soul-searching and damaging period to start rebuilding **your** self-esteem, confidence and life.

As mentioned before, unfortunately this is not a one-off occurrence. You may cycle through this process many times, until all the issues have been addressed to **your** satisfaction.

If you seem to be stuck in any one of these stages, get professional help, do not wait.

"Can I have mine, or do you want both?"

CHAPTER 6

▼

OTHER STRATEGIES (WAYS TO COPE)

Now we have looked at detaching, let's see if there are other things that can be done.

Put Yourself First

Of equal importance to Detaching is the practice of putting yourself first, as soon as you can. Whether you remain together or not, you have learned a very important lesson. You must think of yourself now and **your** future. From now on, put your own interests first in everything you do.

Don't be hasty or in a rush to do anything. Take your time. Think for a while, each and every time. What it is, why are you doing it, what your motivation is and whom are you doing it for. When you have made a decision, sleep on it if you can. Think about it before implementation. If it is not for you or your own good, strongly consider not proceeding and whether you can hand the issue back over!

Dependence v Indepedence v Co-dependence v Undependence v Inter-dependence

It might help to define these relationship principles.

In a brief summary, if you are dependent, you rely on your partner to do things, make decisions and even think for you at times. If you are independent, you make your own decisions and do your own things, sometimes without even asking another's opinions. If you are co-dependent you live your life through other people, making decisions based upon what you think would please your partner or be in her/his best interests, always following her/his lead, not seeming to have a mind or life of your own. There is obviously a great deal more to learn about these traits than my description.

If you are on your own at the moment, and are used to being dependent or depended upon, you may need to learn first to be "undependent," getting used to making decisions and doing things on your own, for yourself, without needing to look to another for support.

Not all of these behaviours are "healthy" for relationships, and it is quite possible to demonstrate more than one. The outcome will all depend on how you interact and what each is looking for from the other. Expectations may have changed during the "Transition" and led to further conflict.

Perhaps the best "solution" to all of this is inter-dependence where you maintain your own independence and rely on your partner in other situations where you both recognise, complement and welcome each other's strengths and weaknesses.

The Oxygen Mask Principle

Remember what the flight attendant tells you about the oxygen mask in the safety briefing on an aeroplane. Put your own on first, to ensure your safety and then look after your children. You must let other adults look after themselves. Exactly the same principle applies here. Do this! You must always look after **yourself** first, at all times!

The Power Of Positive Thought

Don't ever underestimate the power of thinking positively. When we think happy thoughts we become more positive and we show it outwardly. We even project our subconscious and possibly negative feelings to others in the same way. One of the most successful strategies to learn and consider trying is the following:

Whenever a negative thought enters your head just say the word **YES** ten times over. Try not to think of anything else. If possible do this out loud. This accomplishes two things. Firstly, you replace negative thoughts with positive ones and secondly, you will become more positive in your outlook.

So for example, if your partner has said, "I don't want to share a bed with you anymore," imagine a positive consequence if you can as you say the **YES** words. For example, "That means I have even more space to sprawl about and I don't have to put up with your snoring!" Trust me, this strategy works wonders. Just try it yourself!

Recognise Your Limitations

It is very important to recognise and accept your limitations. No matter how much you may wish for a positive change, you have no "super power" to make it happen. Of course, how you react and behave during this "Crisis" may have an effect on the eventual outcome, but do not begin to believe that you have the power to "make it alright" just because you choose to wish and affirm it so.

This goes too for believing in astrological forecasts and the like. Remember that each of these is written generally for one twelfth of the population and could therefore not apply specifically to you, however conveniently written it may sound.

The "No Contact" Strategy

This is a very important strategy, and one that can help you, honestly. It deserves some explanation. Before we start, think of how it is now. Maybe there is constant bickering, fighting, you are always being blamed for everything, walking on "egg shells" and being scared of what is going to be said to you next. You dread the phone to ring or to receive another text or e-mail. Wouldn't it be nice to give yourself a break from all of this?

Well, you can! By properly implementing the "no contact" rules of engagement, you take immediate control of the situation and all future communication.

No contact, strangely enough, does not mean absolutely none at all. What it does mean is that you will set strict boundaries about what subjects are to be discussed and when. Obviously, if you have kids and financial responsibilities, you cannot ignore them or their best interests. For the purposes of explanation, we will refer to these as "business issues."

If you make the very conscious decision not to discuss anything but the "business" related issues with your partner, this is exactly what we are talking about. No more "How are you?" "What have you been up to?" or anything trivial like "How is the weather?" It is neither of your business really, is not helpful and you don't need or want to know. At the same time it is perfectly fine to ask, "How are the kids?" or "What time should I pick them up?" or "Any bills that need sorting out?"

Do not respond to text messages or phone calls that are not specific to these agreed business issues. If you get a message saying "Call me" you may choose to respond, but if you do, be firm and under control in asking, "What do you want to talk about?" and if it is just general chit chat, feel free to say "I am not prepared to talk about that at the moment. Is there anything important to discuss?"

There are tremendous benefits to using "no contact." One of them may be that your partner suddenly realises you are no longer a "pushover" or a "doormat." Your partner will need to have something of importance to speak to you about before trying to make contact. In addition, s/he will be forced into seeing what it is like not having you to chat to, to discuss everyday things with. Your partner might even begin to miss you and make more of an effort, finding real reasons to call you!

This will also show that you are now a stronger person, no longer the weakling s/he thought or made you out to be.

As mentioned before, separating the person from each and every issue will allow you to have time alone, to think, to plan, to handle the situation and regain control of your life.

There is one note to add to the above. S/he might be quite happy with "no contact" with you. S/he won't have to answer to you and after all, s/he might have found someone else to discuss all the day-to-day stuff with but at least it won't do **you** any harm!

Confusing Communication With Contact

You might think, "You have told me to have no contact, but still to keep in contact about the "business issues." Surely we will still be communicating?"

How often have you been told that communication is most important, that you must keep on doing it to keep any hopes of your relationship alive? I want to make a very important point to you here. Communicating by e-mail or letter alone is only a form of keeping contact, of passing information on. It is very "impersonal" and should never be thought of or confused with "personal communication." Without direct vision (if you do meet up,) listening to the sound and inflection of each other's voices (over the telephone,) hearing silences, passion or boredom in the voice, seeing each others eyes, facial and body movements etc. all you can hope to achieve is pass over facts and figures. E-mail will never be a suitable substitute or replacement for personal contact.

So, don't believe that just because you are maintaining "contact" by e-mail that you are "communicating" with each other. Nothing could really be further from the truth.

A Recipe For Success In Dealing With MLC

This section has been adapted from a posting on the midlife forum website. There is no real recipe, not one that you can cook in the kitchen anyway! If only we could boil something up that would make this all work out for the best! To make it stop right now and give us the result we want! However, there are ingredients, which, with practice, can help you find inner peace and strength.

PATIENCE—You will need a large quantity of patience. If you lack this, you will first need to develop it before proceeding with the recipe.

PMA—A consistent Positive Mental Attitude is necessary in dealing with the insanity of your spouse's MLC. Without this ingredient, your recipe will be a failure.

FAITH—You need a strong faith, and to believe this experience is about lessons that some higher power wants you to learn. As with all crisis situations in life, it is where we learn and grow the most. Put your trust in that power. Whatever happens will be what is meant to.

PERSEVERANCE—You will need to find this special ingredient. There will be many times when you want to give up. Without this ingredient you might as well scrap the recipe and ask for a divorce. Perseverance can be found deep within yourself, you just have to look for it.

PRAYERS—If you are religious, you may need a daily dose of prayers. You cannot survive this journey all alone. You need to ask for help. Ask your God or Higher Power to give you the strength to not give up and to guide you on your journey.

LISTENING SKILLS—Good listening skills are necessary for your spouse to trust and be open with you. Do not try and defend yourself, it will just make your spouse withdraw. Remember, you have two eyes, two ears and one mouth. Use them in the same proportion! Look, listen, and speak even more carefully!

LEARNING SKILLS—This recipe would not be complete without good learning skills. You need to read and understand as much as you can about MLC, it will help you to deal with your spouse and be less angry towards them. Knowledge will give you greater strength and make you feel more in control of your life.

EMPATHY—You will need this ingredient as you learn more about MLC, and have a better understanding of the pain and turmoil your spouse is feeling inside.

COMMITMENT—Without a commitment to never, never, ever give up, you will bale out early from all the pain and agony. Remember that there is no gain without pain.

FORGIVENESS—You will need to learn how to forgive your spouse and yourself. "Forgiveness is a gift you give yourself." It is most important to forgive yourself first. You were not to blame for this MLC.

UNCONDITIONAL LOVE—You will have to discover the meaning of unconditional love, that no matter what you or your spouse has done to hurt each other or misbehave during your marriage, you will need to love each other and your-selves unconditionally.

LIFE'S LESSONS—You will need to learn life's lessons. Throughout life, we grow Physically, Emotionally and Spiritually. This MLC experience is a great opportunity for both you and your spouse to grow, and learn all that you are sup-posed to at this stage of life.

LETTING GO—You will need to finally detach or "Let Go" of your spouse. Set her/him free. You have no control over whether s/he returns or not. If s/he decides to return, it could be because of how you have treated and acted towards her/him through her/his MLC journey. By letting go, you will be giving your spouse the space s/he needs to work things out for her~/himself.

TIME—Lots of time is needed for this recipe to work. If you don't give your spouse the proper amount of time s/he needs, you will probably lose your part-ner. It is her/his journey. Your partner is in control of how much time they need. Don't try and rush things. It's probably a good time to toss in another handful of patience, you can never add too much to this recipe.

SENSE OF HUMOUR—After you have found and mixed together all the ingredients listed above, it is time to lighten up and enjoy life. A good sense of humour will get you through the most trying times. Trust me, it doesn't get any-more trying then dealing with a spouse's MLC.

The greatest chance for success with this recipe is to consistently add all of the ingredients. Do not forget any one ingredient, or put too little an amount into the mix. You may need to tweak the recipe to your own taste.

There is no magic ingredient that will cure MLC. It requires a well thought out plan and process to cope properly, with no guarantee of result. There are no shortcuts.

I am going to list ingredients that have been used in past recipes for dealing with MLC. It has been shown that these ingredients do **not** work and should therefore not be used.

DO NOT use these ingredients:

BEGGING, PLEADING, CRYING—Do not use these ingredients, as they have done nothing more than push the spouse with MLC further away.

CONTROL/MANIPULATE—Use of these two ingredients will lead straight to disaster. Trying to control your spouse will make her/him run very fast and far away.

EXPRESSIONS OF LOVE—Stop saying, "I love you", "I miss you" or anything along these lines. These statements put pressure on the MLC'er. Love is an important ingredient, but you must not express it, even if you feel it.

THREATS—Threatening your spouse with divorce will do nothing more than aggravate the situation. It will not make your spouse desire to return home.

FIXING, CHANGING AND CONVINCING YOUR SPOUSE—Forget trying to fix or change your spouse, that's not your job. And this goes for trying to convince your spouse that what s/he is doing is wrong. Save your breath.

ANGER—Do not become angry towards your spouse. Your partner will return you greater anger. Give love and act as if you are happy and life is good to you.

GUILT—Trying to make your spouse feel guilty about leaving you and the kids will not work. Your spouse is very self-centred at this time, s/he only thinks of what s/he wants. Your partner is tired of trying to take care of everyone else's needs while neglecting her/his own.

ACCUSATIONS/BLAMING—Accusing your spouse or blaming her/him for all the problems in your relationship will do no good. Your partner is already convinced that her/his unhappiness in life is because s/he is married to you! So don't go there.

DEFENDING—When your spouse tries to tell you what they don't like about you, don't try and defend yourself. Just sit there and listen, give her/him full eye contact and validate what s/he is saying. You don't have to agree with her/him, but you need to validate that what s/he thinks and feels to her/him is the truth. Whether it is or not does not matter. If you have to, just say, "I am sorry you feel that way" and leave it at that.

An Early Three Step Strategy

Many of the coping strategies may seem complicated on first reading. An alternative is just to make an initial choice from a simple three: Stay, Leave or Wait.

The first decision may be whether you want to **STAY** in the marriage and work it through whatever comes.

The second might be that you have had enough right now and want to **LEAVE** the marriage immediately.

Thirdly, you might want to **WAIT** for a while and see if things improve. It is not that you do not plan for either of the other two options, but your focus will have been removed from either of the others, giving you time to think, plan and focus on you and your needs.

By giving yourself these three immediate choices, you will have given yourself breathing space, shown yourself immediate power and already be in control of your way ahead.

Most importantly, until you have made a decision, **do not** discuss or reveal it to your partner. Remember, **you** are taking control of **your** life, not trying to give her/him more power over you.

Of course, you are allowed to change your mind as circumstances change. But don't do it all the time. You will send all sorts of confusing messages, not only to your partner but also to yourself and those around you.

Other Points To Consider

Blame

As much as we want to, we cannot apportion "blame" to either party, and must not, as much as we might want to. It is important to get to grips with the fact that none of this is either's direct fault. Of course, you are not perfect. No one is, but we need to grow and learn together, accepting each other's imperfections.

The "Bomb"

The "bomb" as it is called, is when one partner tells the other one, "I love you but I am not in love with you," or one of the other classic MLC statements. It normally comes, not right at the beginning of the crisis as you might have expected, but after a period of time in which the person who wishes to leave the relationship has justified to themselves that the time is right and s/he cannot continue as s/he is. This may be up to one or two years after the real start of the "crisis." Remember too that there can be more than one "bomb."

Fog Or Clarity?

There was a discussion on a forum where someone was arguing the case between the two. We like to think of an MLC'er being in a fog throughout her/his "crisis," not knowing which way to turn or what to do. We give her/him the benefit of being in a state of confusion, a "fog." The counter argument is that s/he may not be in a fog at all, but rather have achieved a sense of her/his own clarity, knowing exactly what s/he wants to do, where s/he wants to go and just getting on with it. Maybe you like to see her/him in a fog, or perhaps imagine that you are in that fog, with her/him not being able to see you clearly at the moment.

Just for a moment, think of it from your partner's point of view. Maybe s/he doesn't see a fog at all now. Your partner might have done at some time, throughout her/his indecisive period. At the moment, in your partner's mind s/he can see clearly, perhaps for the first time. Everything seems bright, and your partner thinks that s/he knows what can be seen ahead, all those dreams and opportunities that s/he can make come true. By pushing you to one side s/he can move ahead fast or faster, unhindered by you, hidden in the past. Perhaps this is why s/he has blamed you for all her/his failures. You have stopped her/him from achieving those wonderful goals. As long as s/he can't see you, pretending you don't even exist, s/he thinks only about going straight ahead. This does not mean that her/his crisis is over, just that s/he is progressing through the stages.

Your partner might describe how s/he feels as if being in a fog. One day, s/he comes out of the murk and begins to move forward. I repeat, this does not mean the crisis is over, just that s/he now sees a way forward, whether it is right or wrong. You and the marriage may still be in the fog behind her/him and until s/he chooses to look or go back in to bring you out, that is where you will remain in her/his mind.

So, it may well be that it is only once your partner stops for breath and looks round, whenever s/he does, s/he will see what is left behind or lost or what is being lost wasn't that bad after all. Your partner might start to question her/his motivation and whether what s/he has done is either correct or morally acceptable. Your partner might even choose to reopen negotiations! And it has to be her/him that does this!

People tell us to "never look back." This can be interpreted in so many ways. I like to think of the possibility of saving my relationship in terms of "We will never get **back** together, let's go **forward** together!" Just like memories or habits, keep the good ones and develop new ones as you steam ahead.

Am I Responsible For This?

We all, or nearly all of us, start off by blaming ourselves. What we did wrong. What we could have done. What we needed to change about ourselves and what we were so obviously blind to. Please stop doing this at once! This is not your fault. There is nothing you could have done or can do to prevent or stop this. No matter who your partner would have been with, it is extremely likely that s/he would be in Transition, and the other person might be in a similar "Crisis." And nothing you can do, or change, will make any difference whatsoever. Although I have said this before, whatever you do will not be enough. Another reason for failure will always be found or given.

Don't Take It Personally!

This may seem like a very strange thing to say, and one that might be very difficult to accept. Of course this is highly personal to you, but I am referring here to the way your partner sees the situation.

The best way to describe this theory is to look at the whole picture from a completely detached point of view.

Just for the moment, don't think about your personal relationship. Think of meeting a new person and starting a fresh relationship. (Please don't do it right now, just think about it!) There will be things you like and possibly dislike about the individual. How s/he looks, acts, speaks etc. Only by looking at "the whole package" will you decide whether or not you wish to have any form of relationship with that person. This is exactly what your partner may be doing now.

Now, bring it back to you. Imagine that your partner is viewing you in this way at the moment. There are some things s/he likes about you, but others that s/he doesn't, possibly partly based on past experience and memories, or just expectations. Your partner will judge you for how you are seen now, what s/he thinks you are, not what you have become, or how you might have changed in the interim. In the overall balance, s/he does not wish to be with you at the moment, preferring to keep her/his options open to match current or new wishes. S/he has detached emotionally and now regards you only as a separate person, a virtual stranger, not the partner they are or were committed to spending the rest of her/his life with.

There is nothing "personal" in this. It is just a matter of her/his choice. As hard as it is to accept, you are not the "choice" s/he wishes to make at this time.

However it may feel to you, this is not a "personal" attack on you from her/his point of view. This may help change your perspective on the situation, and help relieve your sensitivity.

Taking v Losing Control

It is very easy to feel out of control, that all decisions are being made for you, that there is nothing **you** can do about it. It is so important to realise that you can only control yourself and what **you** choose to do. Your partner's actions are an important factor, but in no way can or should you try to control them, either now or in the future.

Letting Go

When you are in a committed relationship, you expect to do and share everything together. The fundamental essence of this has now changed. You cannot expect it to be the same. So what do you do, hold on tighter? No, this **never** works, s/he will only run further away. Remember the kite in a strong wind. What happens if you try and pull on the string? Sometimes it will snap and you lose the kite completely. Whereas what would happen if you let out some more string? The kite could still remain attached to you and be retrieved when the wind drops later.

It is the same with a MLC. So, **let go**, however hard it feels and is to do. Your partner needs to be independent, to discover what life is like on her/his own again, so to speak. Your partner needs to see if they miss what they had and whether she or he wants you in the future. If s/he does, an attempt to re-establish contact will be made. If not, that is what s/he wants to do and will continue on that path.

Midlife v Teenage Growth

As mentioned before Midlife is often compared to our teenage year life experiences, trying new things, not committing to one relationship or career, just living life as much as possible, "to the full." Spend a little time remembering what it was like for you and your friends going through those formative years. You may just catch a glimpse of your partner's behaviour and experience a "light-bulb" or have a "Eureka" moment!

Getting Advice

Be very careful who you speak to, what you ask, or expecting others to take your side. Be especially careful of family. Of course your family will support you and possibly some members of your partner's family too.

The biggest problems may arise if you ever do try or manage to reconcile. Those people will know so much about your relationship and what has happened that they might be forever biased towards one or the other of you. They might also know too much about your private life now, and that might be embarrassing for all involved!

You might visit former joint friends on your own and although they might seem to agree with you, it is quite possible that they also concur with and be even closer to your partner. They might just relay part or all of what you say to them, or change the wording slightly or a great deal. You may also, unwittingly put them in the middle and lose their friendship.

For the sake of your ongoing relationship with them, try not to involve them in your personal "Crisis." This is not to say you do not need a close friend at this time. Of course you do. But try and limit what you say to someone you can trust with items of a confidential nature.

Why Do My Friends Tell Me To Leave Her/Him Now?

First of all, remember that they are outside the "triangle" of your relationship and think that they can see things objectively. Second, remember that they are on your side. They only want what they think is best for you. This is why they look for the most straightforward and easy way out, the one that will end your suffering the quickest way possible. They are trying to help.

It may be very frustrating, expecting them to validate your opinions and telling you to carry on fighting to keep the relationship together. But maybe now you can see why they might not.

Remember to do only what you want to do, when you want to. This is **your** life.

Counselling

If you can get counselling, either singly or together, do it. An impartial educated, experienced specially trained listener can help you identify the problems and possible solutions. If your partner refuses to go, do it alone. This will help you cope far better than trying to do it just by yourself with the aid of a book. Try to get a counsellor with experience of MLC, preferably from personal history. S/he will be able to empathise.

Making Mistakes

We all make mistakes. Perhaps you have read some of the things you were "Not supposed to do" and are thinking, "What am I going to do now, that is exactly what I have done!" Don't worry or stress yourself too much, you are learning. Just try not to repeat those mistakes in future.

Doing a 180

It has been recommended too that if what you are or have been doing is having the wrong or no effect at all, it may be worth considering doing the absolute opposite. If what you are doing does not have the desired effect doing more of the same will not do any good. Trying the complete opposite is known as doing a 180. It is very important to note that even this might not work, but you are exploring all the options available to you. Remember you are doing things for **you** now and not for her/him.

For example if you have been clingy, remember to detach. If you have been doing things for her/him that s/he could do her~/himself, stop. If you have been crying in front of her/him, stop. Be happy instead. Obviously you must leave enough time to see if what you are doing is working first! Don't implement a strategy and not follow it through. There would be no point otherwise. And by changing your behaviour completely, even if that feels unnatural at first, you might have a new experience. It goes without saying that you must not do anything illegal or out of spite.

Your spouse might not "believe" what s/he is experiencing because it's so different from the "old" you. Your partner wants to see whether this lasts or you fall back into old behaviours.

But do remember, this is a MLC. There is no guarantee that this activity will bring about miracles!

Realistic expectations

Although it has been stated that a high percentage of relationships survive an MLC I once again cannot confirm that this is correct and do bear in mind that each situation is different in some respects. However, it may give you a glimmer of hope if you think your situation is hopeless at the moment. I also truly believe that it is worth trying to save a relationship, if you want to, for the sake of everyone involved. If something is worth fighting for, "Go for it." However, there does come a time when you realise that banging your head against a brick wall just hurts more and more, and you must remember to look after **yourself** at all times.

Make Decisions And Act On Them!

It is suggested that there is a big "secret" to living life, and that you must make positive decisions, and equally if not more important, act on them. Just making your mind up about what you want to do is not enough. Things don't happen just because you think or wish them to become fact. You can't just let life happen to you. You have to act in a positive way to make it work for you. If you decide what you want to do in the present and for the future, you need to research and implement ways of making it all come true for **you**. No more living in the past, in misery or hope. Draw a line in the sand regarding your situation, accept things for what they really are and start making **your** dreams come true. Only **you** can do it!

Living For Now

This may seem an impossible task, but who knows what tomorrow will bring. It is time to put yourself first, to decide what you want to do, and make definite plans to get on with it.

Take life a little at a time, don't try to do as much as possible all at once. Remember, an hour or day at a time, as referred to elsewhere. Baby steps Rule!

Get A Life!

Have you, like me, been told "Get a life!" And more important than that, how often have you really thought about that statement. You might have taken offence, been insulted, thinking that of course you have a life, or you wouldn't be here in the first place. In fact, this might have been very good advice. You might have been living your life through others, consciously or subconsciously, always placing your own needs and wants second, third or fourth in some cases. You might feel that you lost your own identity and all power in the process.

Well, now you have the chance to put all of this right, placing yourself first, to live your own life for now and the future. You may have been living the life of a "Co-dependent," and I suggest that you read more on that subject too, to understand what you might have been doing and regain control of your life.

Peeling The Onion

To reinforce the principle of dealing with everything a little at a time, think of it as peeling an onion. Only try to deal with one layer at a time. Take a break if and when you need to, then go onto the next one. Eventually you will have uncovered and dealt with everything. (Thanks to "Sparkles" for this one!)

The End Or The Beginning

This may seem like "cold comfort," but it really isn't possible to die from a broken heart, no matter how bad you have been or are feeling. If you cannot save your relationship, try very hard not to think of it as a total loss. Treasure what you have gained from it. Keep only the happy memories. Think of what has happened in a different light. You have learned a great deal about relationships and yourself. You will never make the same mistakes again. You are now a better partner than ever you could have dreamed you would or could be. You are back in control of your own life and destiny. You are being released too. **You** will soon be free!

But I feel In So Much Pain!

Of course you do, we all do. It's just like bereavement. Something has "died" inside us and we are grieving. In order to get over it we have to deal with the pain. And it does happen, in time. There are strategies to help you. Don't try to deal with it all at once. Try and focus on a little bit at a time, a single thought, something you can try to deal with. Take it a little at a time. Give yourself as much time as you need. Do try to set aside a specific time each day, when you can be on your own to process these feelings. Pick a special place where you can relax. Tell yourself; "I am going to allow myself to think about this at such and such a time for quarter or half an hour." Try and limit it to that.

How To Get Support

You may choose to go on the Internet, look up MLC and find a forum or two to read about others' experiences and to voice your own thoughts and concerns. You can and should seek an experienced counsellor to analyse and process your feelings and way forward. Try not to talk to too many people about this. Choose a friend or family member very carefully. You need their confidence, and to be sure they won't talk about it to others, or interfere. This is your problem; even though you didn't create or want it and **you** are the person that has to deal with it. No one else should or can!

Focus On You, You Are A Winner!

Remember that we are trying to get you to change your focus away from the person that has let **you** down. You need to focus on **you**, what **you** want out of life, how **you** are going to get it. Think of it this way, when you pass your (ex) partner on the street in future, have to handle one of their calls or e-mails, you want to be able to think the following: I am going to walk on by calmly, deal with this maturely, thinking and knowing that s/he has lost **me**!

Don't Get Stuck In The Past

Now for something very difficult. I say this because I have done exactly this. It is too easy to think constantly of how good things were and how you want everything "back to normal." We all have to learn, and I know this is repeating myself, that what happened even as recently as yesterday or even an hour ago is now in the past. It is not a bad dream, it is real. Nothing has changed. We cannot alter or revise it. We only have one good and sensible option and that is to live for now and prepare for the future.

It takes a tremendous amount of resolve and a truly conscious decision to put the past behind and to focus exclusively on what we can do. Until we do and take actions accordingly, we continue to "live" on and in past memories and these stop us from going forward. So, as soon as you are able, make a conscious decision to live your life in the present and a forwards direction.

"Yesterday is history, tomorrow is a mystery, today is a gift. That is why it is called the present." The past does not exist, it has gone. The future does not exist, it has not yet arrived. We exist only in the present, in this very moment. This is what all the masters have been teaching … be here and now!

Should I Date Someone Else And When?

If you are no longer with your partner and start to feel lonely, you may be tempted to start dating again. You may be encouraged to go out by friends or family. This may be the basis of a new platonic or sexual relationship for you.

Only you can decide when to start seeing someone else. You may have decided to wait and put your life on hold while the MLC plays itself out. You may restrict your socialising with this in mind, not wanting to prejudice the outcome of your relationship. On the other hand you might accept that your old partnership is over and decide to get on with your life. There should be no restriction of whom you see, when and for what purpose.

Do beware of rebound relationships. You may be expecting too much of your new date/s. You may frighten them off with your expression of needs. You may put them off with talk of the antics or failures of your ex-partner. Try to keep the past where it belongs!

Beware too of the intentions of people you meet. They might seek to take advantage of you, being a vulnerable and emotionally needy person.

Whatever you do, don't go out with someone as a method of revenge against your partner. This can only backfire.

Just be careful and take it slowly. Don't expect everything at once!

"Tough Love"—A Way To Deal With MLC?

There is a strong argument for instigating the use of what is called "Tough Love." This is where you maintain your stance as an adult, specifying what behaviour/s you find acceptable and setting the rules that you expect all parties to comply with. Once you have done this you will be more in control of your life. You will be able to dictate what happens when and where to you. For example, no shouting, swearing or arguing, you will just walk away from any conflict. You certainly won't be the one starting anything!

You may want further explanation. Think of this example of "Tough love." If your teenager comes home and throws up on the carpet, do you run out and buy her or him more drink? Bring this thinking back to you. If your partner is sleeping with another, do you agree to sleep with them straight away again, without at least getting them checked over by a doctor or sex clinic? The key here is to protect yourself at all costs. Don't be responsible for condoning, accepting or even encouraging an unacceptable behaviour pattern.

If you want to find more information on this subject, look for the excellent books by James Dobson.

"Where have **you** been?"

CHAPTER 7

▼

THE END (IS THE SUN COMING OUT AGAIN?)

So, the MLC is coming to an end, or at least you think it is. Time has passed, even if it seems to have dragged by. But the signs are there. The formulae have been followed. What do you do now? Are you still together? Have you made it through this roller coaster ride in separate cars but joined up at the final stop, or have you gone off in totally different directions? Maybe you are talking again. Or maybe you are really together again, trying to repair the damage. It does takes time. An awful lot of it!

How Will I Know When The MLC Is Over?

As said before, this is a very difficult question to answer, not that they all aren't! The first sign may be when your partner starts to want to communicate with you properly, directly, and not through others. When she actually speaks to you, not communicating only by e-mail, by letter or leaving messages when s/he knows you will not be there. When s/he apologises properly for the first time in months or years and is willing to discuss or explain anything you want to know, to your complete satisfaction.

Perhaps one of the clearest signs you will actually be able to see is when your partner or ex-partner stops beginning every sentence or comment by saying I or me, showing her/his concern for you or someone other than her~/himself. As we have seen, during the crisis your partner was always so focussed on her~/himself and what s/he wanted, the mere fact that s/he now sees other people as being important is a very clear step forward.

Reconciling

Reconciliation is no overnight process. Love can grow again. After all, you did not love each other before you met the first time! You can experience a deeper, more meaningful love than ever before, tempered with what you have learned. Trust will have to regained, as well as respect. Some may never manage to do this. In order to do so you have to knock down the walls and barriers you have built in defence and let your guard down again. Is it worth the risk? Only you know the answer. We do know that we never felt so happy or secure as we did when we thought we were in love with that person, so it may well be worth the effort.

There are a lot of questions that will need answers before getting together again. The common term for this is reconciling and there are a lot of points to consider and implement to get it right.

First of all, you both need to show total commitment to each other and your relationship in order to reconcile. Of course you will have many questions of each other. You need to find out whether you both like the "new people."

Don't expect it to be immediate. It takes a long time. Some say it has taken them up to a year or more to openly feel love again.

There is the matter of trust to rebuild and showing full respect to each other. There is no point in starting or continuing if either is not prepared to put one hundred percent of effort into the project.

The MLC'er will have to prove a lot to the LBS'er to make this work. No excuses for past behaviour, just truthful and complete communication starting with a full apology for all the hurt that has been caused. You must not keep on bringing up the past, asking for yet more apologies. If you have had them once, be grateful for them, remember them, and leave it there.

The LBS'er cannot expect the MLC'er to behave as a child anymore. You are both adults and must treat each other as such.

You will have to call on all your reserves to put the past behind you and concentrate on the present and possible future together.

Reconnection

It is widely believed that true reconnection does not begin until near the end of "Withdrawal," when the MLC'er comes to the "Acceptance" stage. Your partner will begin to disassociate with the friends and habits that were acquired during the "Replay" stages. Your partner will begin to dress and act as s/he once did. Your partner may try to meet up if you have been apart and will begin to smile and look you in the eyes again. This will not all occur immediately or simultaneously. Your partner will start to make contact with family and friends from before. The spouse (**you**) will be the last to know!

Your partner might find trivial excuses to speak to or see you. Your partner may now want to find out how you feel about her/him. Your partner might ask if you have found someone new or are in a relationship. At this stage **you** are the one that will make a decision about **your** future. Keep your expectations at zero. Any pressure from you will send her/him straight back into the tunnel. If you want to, treat her/him initially as a potential friend only!

This stage may take a year or longer. Once s/he re-enters your life, if s/he does, it may take another six to nine months for her/him to settle down. Be very careful about what you do or say during this period. Things are **not** back to normal and s/he may run away again!

Many people think that they have experienced signs of reconnection during other stages of MLC. These incidences are not and must not be confused with reconnection. They are or might just be casual checks on you by your partner as time goes by.

Will We Ever Get Together Again?

Unfortunately, I have to state again that there are no guarantees that you will. Both you and your partner will have changed. Although some elements may remain the same, you will be different people in some or many respects. You might not like each other nor wish to spend any time together. You may have forgiven, but be finding it too hard to put your hurt aside. You might both prefer life now with other partners or just want to be alone. Whatever the case, things will never be the same as they were before, they just can't be. After all, you wouldn't want a repeat prescription!

Just because the MLC is over, this does not mean you can resume life together as if nothing has changed. If you choose to, you will both have to address the relationship issues that have come up and need to be resolved.

The "Stranger" Principle

If you are considering getting together and going forward in the future, when the MLC is over, you may well best employ the "Stranger" principle. You are now new people. Even though you knew each other before and you make look the same, you have both changed in many ways. For you to decide to venture forth together you need to start dating each other anew. Don't take things too fast. Don't expect things to "get back to normal." That "normal" is in the past. Get to know each other again, as if meeting for the first time. Don't rush things. You may just push your "potential partner" away again, inadvertently.

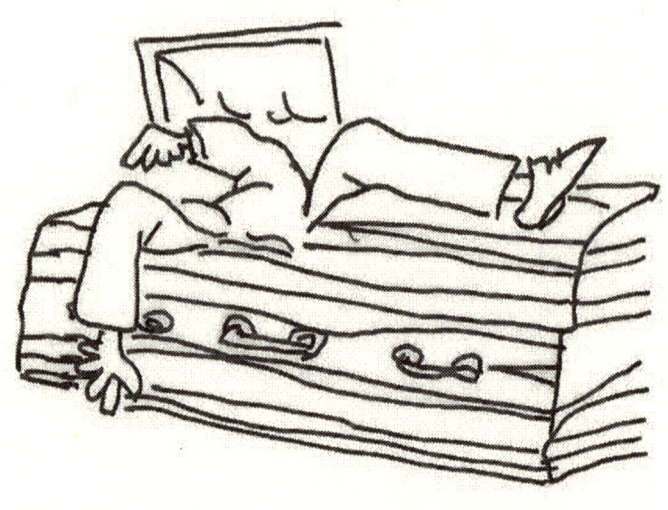

"Time to get up and live, **again**!"

CHAPTER 8

▼

AFTER THE END (IS THERE LIFE AFTER THE "DEATH?")

So what do you do now? Is there anything worth saving? Can you even talk to each other anymore? Do you both agree to go together for counselling? Are you both truly committed to making things better? Or, are you now on your own? Very importantly, do **you** actually want to get together anew with this man or woman?

An important mindset to get into is that you will not be going back. You must go **forward**, with or without this person. If you do, you will never be the same couple you once were. That is all in the past, and that is where it must remain.

Whatever you are experiencing now has to be better than what you have endured for the time you have. Some may experience a life and love like never before, with the existing (but new) partner or maybe someone totally new. Some may be doing something totally different with their lives or living in another place. Whatever has happened, you have learned a lot, about yourself and other people. You certainly know a lot more about relationships and what makes people tick. You may have discovered a new vocation, new skills or hobbies, and who your real friends are. Whatever, **you** are on the track upwards now, with no hidden bends or dark tunnels.

Your Own Awakening

We have talked about the MLC'er "Waking up," but what about you? It might be hard to take this on board now, but in time you will realise many things that assist in your own "Awakening." They might not all happen at once, but you can compile and tick off your own recovery list.

You will:

- Accept what has happened and stop questioning it.

- Stop over-analysing your situation and the part you think you played.

- Stop blaming yourself.

- Realise that whatever there was between the two of you is well and truly over and in the past.

- Accept that there is no worthy current partnership between the two of you.

- Understand that you may or may not be together in the future.

- Not put your faith in false hopes.

- Understand that nothing **you** can do will make things right.

- Know that **you** cannot control the actions of others.

- Understand that only **you** are responsible for your own future.

- Start to have more happy than sad days or moments.

- Want to go out and socialise again, with old and new friends.

- Not want to go over and over old ground with friends and associates.

- Know that if you are approached to reconcile, the decision will be **yours**.

- Know and accept that "**What will be will be.**"

- Remember; "**If it is to be, it is up to me.**"

CHAPTER 9

▼

ABBREVIATIONS, QUOTES AND JOKES

It might help you to include a list of common Internet abbreviations, and quotes and jokes that might give you a little lift, after the hard slog of reading this short tome. I hope that they will be of use and bring you some joy.

Common Abbreviations Used In MLC Internet Chat

When you do talk on a forum, many people use abbreviations. Too many actually! This list is by no means comprehensive. There are new ones added all the time, but this will give you a head start:

24/7 or 24-7	—	All the time
A	—	Affair
AAMOF	—	As A Matter Of Fact
AD	—	Anti Depressants
AFAIK	—	As Far As I Know
AFK	—	Away From Keyboard
AKA	—	Also Known As
ASAP	—	As Soon As Possible
ATM	—	At The Moment
AYOR	—	At Your Own Risk
BLX	—	Bollocks!
B2U	—	Back To You
B4	—	Before
BAIC	—	Boy Am I Confused
BAK	—	Back At Keyboard
BBL	—	Be Back Later
BBS	—	Be Back Soon
B/C	—	Because
BCNU	—	Be Seeing You
BF	—	Boyfriend
BFD	—	Big F***ing Deal
BFN	—	Bye For Now
BG or <bg>	—	Big Grin

BIL	—	Brother-In-Law
BOB	—	Battery-Operated-Boyfriend
BOT	—	Back On Topic
BRB	—	Be Right Back
BRT	—	Be Right There
BS	—	Betrayed Spouse
BTA	—	But Then Again …
BTDT	—	Been There Done That
BTU	—	Back To You
BTW	—	By The Way
BWL	—	Busting With Laughter
BWTHDIK	—	But What The Heck Do I Know?
BYKT	—	But You Knew That
BYTM	—	Better You Than Me
CMIIW	—	Correct Me If I'm Wrong
CRB	—	Come Right Back
CRBT	—	Crying Real Big Tears
CU	—	See You
CWOT	—	Complete Waste Of Time
CYA	—	Cover Your A**
C YA L8R	—	See you later
CYWW2BY	—	See Ya, Wouldn't Want To Be Ya
D	—	Divorce

D(Number)	—	Daughter, Age
DBD	—	Day By Day
DD	—	Dear Daughter
DH	—	Dear Husband
DHYB	—	Don't Hold Your Breath
DIAFYO	—	Did I Ask For Your Opinion?
DIIK	—	Darned If I Know
DIKU	—	Do I Know You?
DIL	—	Daughter-In-Law
DILLIGAF	—	Do I Look Like I Give A F***?
DITYID	—	Did I Tell You I'm Distressed?
DIY	—	Do It Yourself
DMMGPOU	—	Don't Make Me Go Postal On U
DOM	—	Dirty Old Man
DQMOT	—	Don't Quote Me On This
DTRT	—	Do The Right Thing
DW	—	Dear Wife
DYJHIW	—	Don't You Just Hate It When …
EA	—	Emotional Affair
EG or <eg>	—	Evil Grin
EMA	—	Extramarital Affair
EMFBI	—	Excuse Me For Butting In
EOD	—	End Of Discussion
EOR	—	End Of Rant

EZ	—	Easy
F2F	—	Face to Face
FAQ	—	Frequently Asked Questions
FIL	—	Father-In-Law
FOMCL	—	Falling Off My Chair Laughing
FTBOMH	—	From The Bottom Of My Heart
FTR	—	For The Record
FUBAR	—	Fouled Up Beyond All Recognition
FUT	—	Follow Up To
FWIW	—	For What It's Worth
FYA	—	For Your Amusement
FYI	—	For Your Information
G or <g>	—	Grin
GA	—	Go Ahead
GAL	—	Get A Life
GBH	—	Great Big Hug
GBH&K	—	Great Big Hug & Kiss
GF	—	Girlfriend
GFN	—	Gone For Now
GG	—	Good Game
GIGO	—	Garbage In, Garbage Out
GL	—	Good Luck
GMAB	—	Give Me A Break

GMTA	—	Great Minds Think Alike
GOL	—	Giggling Out Loud
GR&D	—	Grinning, Running & Ducking
GTG	—	Got To Go
H	—	Husband
HAND	—	Have A Nice Day
HB	—	Hug Back
HH	—	Holding Hands
HHIS	—	Hanging Head In Shame
HHOJ	—	Ha Ha, Only Joking
HHOK	—	Ha Ha, Only Kidding
HHOS	—	Ha Ha, Only Serious
HIT	—	Hang In There
HIWTH	—	Hate It When That Happens
HOS	—	Husband Over Shoulder
HTH	—	Hope That Helps
IAC	—	In Any Case
IAE	—	In Any Event
IANAL	—	I Am Not A Lawyer
IAOFN	—	I Am On Fire Now
IAWTP	—	I Agree With This Post
IC	—	Individual Counseling
ICOCBW	—	I Could, Of Course, Be Wrong

ICTTAM	—	I Cant Take This Any More
IDGI	—	I Don't Get It
IDGRA	—	I Don't Give A Rat's A**
IDK	—	I Don't Know
IDTS	—	I Don't Think So
IDKWUM	—	I Don't Know What You Mean
IIRC	—	If I Recall Correctly
IKWUM	—	I Know What You Mean
IYKWIM	—	If You Know What I Mean
ILAT	—	I Laughed At That
IMCO	—	In My Considered Opinion
IME	—	In My Experience
IMHO	—	In My Humble Opinion
IMNSHO	—	In My Not-So-Humble Opinion
IMO	—	In My Opinion
IMS	—	I am Sorry
IO	—	Information Overload
IOW	—	In Other Words
IRL	—	In Real Life
ISO	—	In Search Of
ITT	—	It's The Truth
J4G	—	Just For Grins
J4U	—	Just For You
JAM	—	Just A Minute

JASE	—	Just Another System Error
JAT	—	Just A Thought
JIC	—	Just In Case
JIT	—	Just In Time
JK	—	Just Kidding
JMO	—	Just My Opinion
JOOC	—	Just Out Of Curiosity
JTLYK	—	Just To Let You Know
KISS	—	Keep It Simple, Stupid
KIT	—	Keep In Touch
KOTC	—	Kiss On The Cheek
KWIM	—	Know What I Mean?
KYTS	—	Keep Your Trap Shut
LBS	—	Left Behind Spouse
LDR	—	Long Distance Relationship
LI	—	Laughing Inside
LIS	—	Laughing In Silence
LOL	—	Laughing Out Loud
LMAO	—	Laughing My A** Off
LMFAO	—	Laughing My F*****g A*** Off
LTR	—	Long Term Relationship
LYLAB/S	—	Love You Like A Brother/Sister

MC	—	Marriage Counseling
MIL	—	Mother-In-Law
MOM	—	Married Other Man
MOO	—	My Own Opinion
MOP	—	Married Other Person
MOTOS	—	Members Of The Opposite Sex
MOTSS	—	Members Of The Same Sex
MOW	—	Married Other Woman
MYOB	—	Mind Your Own Business
MYOFB	—	Mind Your Own F*****g Business
NIFOC	—	Naked In Front Of Computer
NLOYB	—	No Longer Any Of Your Business
NOTTOMH	—	Not Off The Top Of My Head
NOYB	—	None Of Your Business
NOYBB	—	None Of Your Bloody Business
NOYFB	—	None Of Your Fucking Business
NP	—	No Problem
NRN	—	No Reply Necessary
NSISR	—	Not Sure If Spelled Right
OBTW	—	Oh, By The Way
OG	—	Other Girl
OIC	—	Oh, I See!
OLL	—	Online Love

OM	—	Other Man
OMG	—	Oh My God
OP	—	Other Person
OT	—	Off Topic
OTOH	—	On The Other Hand
OTT	—	Over The Top
OW	—	Other Woman
PA	—	Physical Affair
PDA	—	Public Display of Affection
PITA	—	Pain In The A**
PM	—	Private Message
PMJI	—	Pardon Me, Jumping In (when you interrupt)
PM4JI	—	Same as above
PMFJI	—	Pardon Me For Jumping In (same as above)
PMFI	—	Same as above
PMSL	—	Pissing/peeing Myself Laughing
POTC	—	Peck On The Cheek
POV	—	Point Of View
PYSIMP	—	Put Yourself In My Place
QFT	—	Quote For Truth
R	—	Relationship

R	—	Reconciliation
R & D	—	Research and Development
RB	—	Reality Bites
REHI	—	Hello Again
RL	—	Real Life
ROFL	—	Rolling On the Floor Laughing
ROFLMAO	—	Rolling On the Floor Laughing My Ass Off
RSN	—	Real Soon Now
RT	—	Real Time
RUOK	—	Are You OK?
RW	—	Real World
RX	—	Prescription
S	—	Smile
S(Number)	—	Son, Age
SA	—	Sexual Affair
SB	—	Smiles Back
SIL	—	Sister-In-Law
SIL	—	Son-In-Law
SITD	—	Still In The Dark
SIUYA	—	Stick It Up Your Arse
SNAFU	—	Situation Normal, All Fouled Up
SNMP	—	So Not My Problem
SO	—	Significant Other
SOB	—	Son Of A B****

SOL	—	S*** Outta Luck
SOS	—	Same Old Stuff
SOS	—	Someone Over Shoulder
SOSG	—	Someone Over Shoulder Gone
SOSO	—	Same Old, Same Old
STBX	—	Soon-To-Be-Ex
STBXH	—	Soon-To-Be-Ex Husband
STBXW	—	Soon-To-Be-Ex Wife
SU	—	Shut Up
SYL	—	See You Later
TAL	—	Thanks A Lot
TBH	—	To Be Honest
TCO	—	Taken Care Of
TCOB	—	Taking Care Of Business
TCOY	—	Take Care Of Yourself
TEOTWAWKI	—	The End Of The World As We Know It
TFE	—	Thanks For Everything
TFH	—	Thread From Hell
THX	—	Thanks
TIA	—	Thanks In Advance
TIC	—	Tongue In Cheek
TILII	—	Tell It Like It Is
TIS	—	That Is Sooooooo
TMI	—	Too Much Information

TOW	—	The Other Woman
TPME	—	That Pisses Me Off
TTBOMK	—	To The Best Of My Knowledge
TTFN	—	Ta Ta For Now
TTT	—	Thought That, Too
TTYL	—	Talk To You Later
TTYS	—	Talk To You Soon
UKWIS	—	You Know What I'm Saying
UMMD!	—	You Made My Day!
URAQT	—	You Are A Cutie
URSW	—	You Are So Wise
VBG or <vbg>	—	Very Big Grin
W	—	Wife
W/E	—	Whatever
WEG or <weg>	—	Wide Evil Grin
WG or <wg>	—	Wicked Grin
WOS	—	Wife Over Shoulder
WP	—	Wrong Person
WRT	—	With Regard To
WS	—	Wayward Spouse
WTF	—	What The F**k
WTFIGOH	—	What the F**k Is Going On Here

WTG	—	Way To Go!
WTH	—	What The Heck
WTHDTM	—	What The Heck Does That Mean
WYSIWYG	—	What You See Is What You Get
X	—	Ex
XH	—	Ex-Husband
XW	—	Ex-Wife
YMMV	—	Your Mileage May Vary
YMMVG	—	Your Mileage May Vary Greatly

<u>Your Guide To E-Mail Emoticons</u>

Remember that most of these need to be read sideways, or they don't make sense.

A

0=)	Angel
:-t	Angry

B

~:0	Baby
:-o	Bored
:-#	Braces
</3	Broken Heart

C

=^.^=	Cat
:0)	Clown
0.o	Confused
:-S	Confused
B-)	Cool
):-(	Cranky face
: (	Crying
:'(	Crying

D

_	Dazed
#-o	Doh!
:*)	Drunk

E

-@—@-	Eyeglasses

F

<(*_*)>	Face
<OOO<<	Fish
0—<	Fishy
()	Football
:-(	Frown
:(	Frown
=P	Frustrated
:-P	Frustrated

G

$_$	Greedy
:->	Grin

H

=)	Happy
:-)	Happy
:)	Happy
d:)	Happy with baseball cap
<3	Heart
:l	Hmm face
(:(l)	Homer
(8^(l)	Homer
{}	Hug

I

:-l	Indifferent

J

X-p	Joking
K	
\VVV/	King
L	
=D	Laughing Out Loud
)-:	Left handed sad face
(-:	Left handed smiley face
M	
=/	Mad
@@@8^)	Marge Simpson
:-) (-:	Married
<:3)~	Mouse
N	
~.~	Napping
:-B	Nerd
O	
^_^	Overjoyed
P	
<1:0	Partying
:-/	Perplexed
0#<	Person
=8)	Pig
%==>	Prick or Penis
%==>~	Prick or Penis with Come
(#*__*#)	Pretty

\&&&/	Princess
Q	
\&&&/	Queen
R	
:=D	Really Happy
@~)~~	Rose (Or Any Flower)
S	
=(	Sad
:-(	Sad
:(	Sad
:*(	Sad face with tear
:-7	Sarcastic
:-@	Screaming
O-/<]	Skateboarder
0[-<l	Skater
:-)	Smile
:-Q	Smoking
:>	Smug
:P	Sticking Tongue Out
~o—~	Swimming
:o	Surprised
T	
:-{}	Talking
(:I	Tired
:-J	Tongue In Cheek

:-&	Tongue Tied
U	
=-O	Uh-oh
:-/	Undecided
****_	US Flag
V	
:-E	Vampire
W	
8-)	Wearing Sunglasses
: ----)?	Why the long face?
;-)	Winking
;)	Winking

A Few Jokes And Quotes To Liven Up Your Day

Some Simply Stupid Actual Statements Made By MLC'ers

"I don't need life insurance anymore. If I die, you can look after the kids."

"I need my passport back … and my skis"

"I never loved you. You forced me into marriage."

"You give and you take, but you never give."

"Sometimes I confuse myself …"

"I'm leaving at 2.30 or 3.30, whichever comes first."

"I know who she is, but I just can't tell you."

"I need to ask my girlfriend's husband."

"I think I better pull my pants up …"

"Sometimes I get confused with names."

"Quit leaving voicemail messages on my answer machine."

"I'm just thinking in my head."

"I decided our marriage was over in my head before I started my affair."

"I don't think you should have to work at a relationship."

"Marriage is just a piece of paper."

"Marriage is a contract and should be renewed every 10 yrs with an opt out option."

"I don't have any regrets."

"I never said that."

"I hope we can stay friends. I never meant to hurt you."

"I never said that I loved you."

"We have changed, we aren't the same people anymore" … then in the next breath … "People don't change … they always stay the same."

"Maybe we should look at our marriage in a different way."

"Change jobs … he said … that's just stupid … I change jobs … and we still don't work out … then I would be stuck in a job I didn't want to be in."

"I HAD to leave this weekend, because you threatened to cancel all the credit cards!"

"You know I'm not an alcoholic anymore, and I was only an alcoholic while I was married to you, so that means YOU made me an alcoholic".

"You like to cook, I don't like food or eating."

"He said that he bought a Harley for my birthday. I can't even drive a motorcycle."

"If you were more committed to our marriage, you would have cooked more vegetables."

Just Stupid Things People Say—No Relevance To MLC

To relieve the tension even more and just put in a list of some stupid things people say:

1. People who point at their wrist while asking for the time. "I know where my watch is pal. Where is yours? Do I point at my crotch when I ask for the toilet?"

2. People who are willing to get off their arse to search the entire room for the TV remote because they refuse to walk to the TV and change the channel manually!

3. When people say "Oh, you just want to have your cake and eat it too. Of course! What good is a cake if you can't eat it?"

4. When people say "It's always the last place you look". Of course it is! Why would you keep looking after you've found it? Do people actually do this? Who and where are they?

5. When people say while watching a film "Did you see that"? No, I paid £8 to come to the cinema and stare at the floor.

6. People who ask "Can I ask you a question?" Didn't really give me a choice there, did you?

7. When something is "New and Improved!" Which is it? If it's new, then there has never been anything before it. If it's an improvement, then there must have been something wrong with it before!

8. When people say "Life is too short." What the hell? Life is the longest damn thing you will ever do! What can tell you me that is longer?

9. When you are waiting for the bus and someone asks "Has the bus come yet?" If the bus had come already, would I be standing here?

10. People who say things like "My eyes aren't what they used to be." So what were they before, ears?

11. When you're eating something and someone asks "Is that nice?" "No, it's really revolting. I always eat stuff I hate."

Anonymous Quotes

"I recently read that love is entirely a matter of chemistry. That must be why my spouse treats me like toxic waste."

* * * *

"When a man steals your wife or a woman steals your husband, there is no better revenge than to let them keep them."

* * * *

"After marriage and going through MLC, husband and wife can become two sides of a coin; they just can't face each other, but may still stay together."

* * * *

"By all means marry. If you get a good spouse, you'll be happy. If you get a bad one, you'll become a philosopher."

* * * *

"I had some words with my MLC partner, and my partner had some paragraphs with me."

* * * *

"The secret of a long marriage. Go to a restaurant two times a week with a little candlelight, dinner, soft music and dancing. You go on Tuesdays, your partner on Fridays."

*   *   *   *

"I don't worry about terrorism anymore. I was married for ten years."

*   *   *   *

"There's a way of transferring funds that is even faster than electronic banking. It's called marriage."

*   *   *   *

"I've had bad luck with both my spouses. The first one left me, and the second one didn't."

*   *   *   *

"Two secrets to keep your marriage brimming:
1. Whenever you're wrong, admit it,
2. Whenever you're right, shut up."

*   *   *   *

"The most effective way to remember your spouse's birthday is to forget it once."

*   *   *   *

"You know what I did before I married? Anything I wanted to."

*   *   *   *

"My wife and I were happy for twenty years. Then we met."

＊   ＊   ＊   ＊

"Marriage is the only war where one sleeps with the enemy."

Marital Jokes

Husband: When I get mad at you, you never fight back. How do you control your anger? Wife: I clean the toilet bowl. Husband: How does that help? Wife: I use your toothbrush!

*   *   *   *

A husband and wife come to counselling after 15 years of marriage. When asked what the problem was, the wife went into a passionate, painful tirade listing every problem they had ever had in the 15 years they had been married. She went on and on: neglect, lack of intimacy, emptiness, loneliness, feeling unloved and unlovable, an entire laundry list of unmet needs she had endured over the course of their marriage.

Finally, after allowing this to go on for a sufficient length of time, the therapist got up, walked around the desk and, after asking the wife to stand, embraced and kissed her passionately. The woman shut up and quietly sat down as if in a daze. The therapist turned to the husband and said, "This is what your wife needs at least three times a week. Can you do this?"

The husband thought for a moment and replied "Well, I can drop her off Mondays and Wednesdays, but on Fridays, I fish."

*   *   *   *

Husband was caught shoplifting a can of peaches. When they found him he was just finished eating the last one. The judge asked him if he ate the peaches. He said yes, they were quite good. The judge asked how many peaches were in the can. Seven he replied. The judge said you will spend one night in jail for each peach, so your sentence will be seven days. Just as the judge was ready to bang his gavel, the wife stood up and yelled "Wait, he stole a can of peas too!"

*   *   *   *

An old man goes to a wizard to ask him to remove a curse under which he has been living for 40 years. The wizard says, "Perhaps, but you will have to tell me the exact words that were used to put you under that curse." The old man says, "I pronounce you man and wife."

*   *   *   *

A man whose credit cards were stolen says he won't report it to the police because the thief is spending less on them than his wife did.

"**Please** tell me this is over!"

CHAPTER 10

▼

FINALE

Well, we have come to the end of our brief guide to MLC. I hope you now feel better able to cope with what you are experiencing.

My dearest wish is that you understand what you and your partner are going through now. I do hope that you are able to resolve your differences and if you both wish to, carry on or start again together in a more fulfilling and loving relationship.

If you are single and starting again, remember that you are now a more developed person. **You** know so much more about human nature. **You** will have clearly defined aims, objectives and standards for your next relationship. **You** will have learned what works and what doesn't. **You** will have one when you are ready. Have no doubt. There are many truly compatible companions in the world for **you**. There is nothing wrong with **you**. **You** have so much to offer, even more than before!

Maybe you also agree with me now that this may be better described as a "Kamikaze" experience. Either way, it is not pleasant for any of us, not for a minute. But we do learn from life, both the happy and sad experiences. After all, when it comes down to it we are only human and only live once. What we do with our time here is up to us. Remember, and use this as your personal motto:

"IF IT IS TO BE, IT IS UP TO ME!"

"I think we need a drink now!"

A Final Laugh

List Of Made Up Reviewer Comments:

"This is a load of Midlife Lousy Crap!"
"This is a simple book, written in a simple way, for simple people. Quite simply!"
"The shortest, best way to get a hangover without drinking!"
"The best book for your toilet read that I have read in a long while!"
"And I thought it was safe to get married!"
"You can read it in the bathtub—and it will soak you up completely"
"Best read in isolation, preferably solitary confinement!"
"This book promises nothing it can't deliver. And it doesn't!"

List Of Made Up Reviews by MLC'ers

"MLC Review—I have nothing to say. You may quote me."
"MLC Review—I never read this, and I am not going to. I am not in MLC"
"MLC Review—I never meant to hurt you, why did you take it personally?"
"MLC Review—Does this book make me look old or fat?"
"MLC Review—Did I say that? I don't remember."
"MLC Review—I want to halve the royalties, give me your half and I will keep mine."

Update (June 2007)

Since starting to write this book, I have learned so much more, not only from the experience itself but also from a lot of others. Thank you everyone! I still believe that everything I have written is highly relevant and would like to give you an update on my personal situation.

It is now 15 months since I received the initial "bomb" by e-mail and I am no longer in regular contact with my (ex) partner. No more phone calls or personal contact, just the occasional e-mail about "business" issues, nothing substantial for two months now. I still visit our children every now and then, but do not see my STBXW (soon to be ex-wife) at all. She has cut off all contact and chooses not to be around or available. Although requested by her, I refused to be the one petitioning for divorce, so she is applying on the basis of "Marriage Breakdown."

A few months have passed and I have still to hear from her lawyer, so am waiting anxiously for "that" letter to drop through the mailbox. I still love her and have always wanted to maintain as close a friendship as I can so that there may be an element of chance for us after the "Crisis" has done its damage and disappeared. To date she has told me that this is not possible, certainly from her side, and we are not even "friends" anymore.

I have just started to go through periods where I congratulate myself for feeling fully detached, but at times I still feel down and sorry for myself again, especially in the evenings, at weekends and on birthdays. It has been a very long 15 months, and this ties in so closely with the management of grief (as discussed.) I know now that the ups will get more than the downs as time goes on. I used to get so annoyed when others told me "Give it time," but I am testament to the fact that this is becoming true. Things are getting better, and I feel a lot happier than I have in what seems like years. I have actually been out on "dates," but I have to admit I felt rather guilty throughout, even though nothing "happened."

Let me finish this by coming back to my own "Transition." If I believe my own words and conclusions (which I choose to,) I began my Transition at around the age of forty-two. I am coming up to forty-nine now and honestly think I am reaching the end of it. It is ending with a whimper, not a bang! So I was a full "seven-yearer." It has not been easy. I can see many things so clearly now that I could not even rationalise before. I have reached a balance between the "material" and "ethereal" world that I could not mix and match together properly in the past. I understand myself and my (ex) partner so much better. I have matured. I too have grown up. It is as if we were both on the same point on a circle, then I moved one way, and a little later my partner set off the other way. We both had different things to learn about life and love, and set off on different paths to achieve what we needed. I have no doubt that at some time in the future we will meet up and start communicating again, but whether it is to be together again or not I do not know and cannot say.

About the Author

Flash! is a 48 year-old male, father of two who lives in the United Kingdom. With a BSc in Marketing and Business, he has worked in the Healthcare market for many years. He has been married once, for 13 years. Recently suffering a marriage breakdown, which he believes may be due in part to his own transition and a "Crisis" experienced by his wife, he has coached many others through MLC and decided to put fingers to keyboard to help others try to come to terms with the devastation this brings to our lives.

Index Of Selected Questions

	Page
Will I Find All The Answers Here?	3
Will The Answers Given Really Apply To Me?	4
Should I Let My Partner Read It?	5
Is Midlife Crisis Really Responsible For What Is Happening?	6
Whose Crisis Is It Anyway?	10
When Does It Happen?	10
What Causes MLC To Happen In The First Place?	11
Is MLC Real Or Imaginary?	12
Is MLC An Illness?	12
Anything I Can Do? I Want To Help!	13
Why Me? What Did I Do To Deserve This?	14
What Should I Be Feeling?	14
What Are Some Other Symptoms I Might Experience?	15
Why Do I Feel As If I Am Living In A Dream?	15
Why Do I Feel As If I Have "Died?"	16
Why Is The Other Person So Different To Me?	18
Why Is S/he Spending So Much Money?	19

Does S/he Experience Memory Loss?   19

Do I Need To Apologise?   19

Will S/he Ever Come Out Of This?   20

How Long Does It Last?   21

Will S/He Ever Be The Same Again?   21

Will There Be Any Regrets?   21

Why Don't I Feel Like Doing Anything?   22

How Can I Stop Thinking About This? It Hurts So Much!   22

Why Can't I Sleep Properly?   23

So Why Do I Want to Sleep All The Time?   23

What Is MLC. Is It Real?   24

Why Am I Putting Myself Through This?   25

How Will I Know When It Is Over?   26

How Long Will It Take Me To Get Over This?   26

Why Won't S/he Speak To Me?   58

Why Doesn't S/he Want To See Me?   59

Why Does S/he Still Want To Be "Friends?"   59

Why Does S/he Say That S/he Wants Me To Get On   60
With My Own Life?

Why Does S/he Say S/he Can't Be Her~/himself When S/   61
he Is With Me?

How Long Does The Crisis Last?   64

Can MLC Be Prevented?   64

What Is Detaching?   74

Am I Responsible For This?   94

Why Do My Friends Tell Me To Leave Her/him Now?   96

Should I Date Someone Else And When?   101

Will We Ever Get Together Again?   106

978-0-595-44087-0
0-595-44087-8

www.ingramcontent.com/pod-product-compliance
Lightning Source LLC
Chambersburg PA
CBHW020431290526
45785CB00002B/789